The Evidence in the Case

By James M. Beck and Joseph H. Choate

INTRODUCTION

BY THE HON. JOSEPH H. CHOATE, FORMER AMERICAN AMBASSADOR TO GREAT BRITAIN[1]

[Footnote 1: Reprinted, by permission, from the N. Y. Times.]

For five months now all people who read at all have been reading about the horrible war that is devastating Europe and shedding the best blood of the people of five great nations. In fact, they have had no time to read anything else, and everything that is published about it is seized upon with great avidity. No wonder, then, that Mr. James M. Beck's book, The Evidence in the Case, published by G. P. Putnam's Sons, which has grown out of the article by him contributed to the New York Times Sunday Magazine, has been warmly welcomed both here and in England as a valuable addition to the literature of the day.

An able and clear-headed lawyer and advocate, he presents the matter in the unique form of a legal argument, based upon an analysis of the diplomatic records submitted by England, Germany, Russia, France, and Belgium, as "A Case in the Supreme Court of Civilization," and the conclusions to be deduced as to the moral responsibility for the war.

The whole argument is founded upon the idea that there is such a thing as a public conscience of the world, which must and will necessarily pass final judgment upon the conduct of the parties concerned in this infernal struggle. Many times in the course of the book he refers emphatically to that "decent respect to the opinions of mankind" to which Jefferson appealed in our Declaration of Independence as the final arbiter upon our conduct in throwing off the British yoke and declaring our right to be an independent nation. That this "public opinion of the world" is the final tribunal upon all great international contests is illustrated by the fact that all mankind, including Great Britain herself, has long ago adjudged that our great Declaration was not only just, but necessary for the progress of mankind.

It is evident from his brief preface that Mr. Beck is a sincere admirer of historic Germany, and on the eve of the war he was at Weimar, after a brief visit to a little village near Erfurt, where one of his ancestors was born, who had migrated at an early date to Pennsylvania, a Commonwealth whose founder had made a treaty with the Indians which, so far from being treated as a "mere scrap of paper," was never broken. Like many Americans, Mr. Beck is of mixed ancestry, being in part English and in part Swiss-German. He has therefore viewed the great question objectively, and without any racial prejudice.

A careful study of the diplomatic correspondence that preceded the outbreak of the war had convinced Mr. Beck that Germany was chiefly responsible for it, and he proceeds con amore to demonstrate the truth of this conviction by the most earnest and forceful presentation of the case.

Forensic lawyers in the cases they present are about half the time on the wrong side, or what proves by the final judgment to have been the wrong side, but it is always easy to tell from the manner of presentation whether they themselves are thoroughly convinced of the justice of the side which they advocate. It is evident that Mr. Beck did not undertake to convince "the Supreme Court of Civilization" until he was himself thoroughly persuaded of the justice of his cause, that the invasion of Belgium by Germany was not only a gross breach of existing treaties, but was in violation of settled international law, and a crime against humanity never to be forgotten, a crime which converted that peaceful and prosperous country into a human slaughterhouse, reeking with the blood of four great nations. How any intelligent lawyer could have come to any other conclusion it is not easy to imagine, since Germany confessed its crime while in the very act of committing it, for on the very day that the German troops crossed the Belgian frontier and hostilities began, the Imperial Chancellor at the great session of the Reichstag on August 4th declared, to use his own words:

Necessity knows no law. Our troops have occupied Luxemburg, and have possibly already entered on Belgian soil. That is a breach of international law.... We were forced to ignore the rightful protests of the Governments of Luxemburg and Belgium, and the injustice--I speak openly--the injustice we thereby commit, we will try to make good as soon as our military aims have been attained. Anybody who is threatened as we are threatened and is fighting for his highest possessions can have only one thought--how he is to hack his way through.

Thank God, their military aims have not yet been attained, and from present appearances are not likely to be, but, as Mr. Beck believes, Germany will still be held by the judgment of mankind to make good the damage done.

In reviewing the diplomatic correspondence published by Germany that preceded the outbreak of the war, Mr. Beck lays great stress, and we think justly, upon the obvious suppression of evidence by Germany, in omitting substantially all the important correspondence on vital points that passed between Germany and Austria, and the suppression of important evidence in judicial proceedings always carries irresistible weight against the party guilty of it. While England and France and Russia were pressing Germany to influence and control Austria in the interests of peace, not a word is disclosed of what, if anything, the German Foreign Office said to Austria toward that end. To quote Mr. Beck's own words:

Among the twenty-seven communications appended to the German White Paper, it is most significant that not a single communication is given of the many which passed from the Foreign Office of Berlin to that of Vienna, and only two which passed from the German Ambassador in Vienna to the German Chancellor, and the purpose of this suppression is even more clearly indicated by the complete failure of Austria to submit any of its diplomatic records to the scrutiny of a candid world.

Notwithstanding the disavowal given by the German Ambassador at Petrograd to the Russian Minister of Foreign Affairs, that the German Government had no knowledge of the text of the Austrian note before it was handed in, and did not exercise any influence on its contents, Mr. Beck establishes clearly by the admissions of the German Foreign Office itself that it was consulted by Austria previous to the ultimatum, and that it not only approved of its course, but literally gave to Austria carte blanche to proceed. And the German Ambassador to the United States formally admitted in an article in The Independent of September 7, 1914, that "Germany had approved in advance the Austrian ultimatum to Servia."

This brutal ultimatum by a great nation of fifty millions of people, making impossible demands against a little one of four millions which had itself just emerged from two conflicts and was still suffering from exhaustion--an ultimatum which set all the nations of Europe in agitation--is proved to have been jointly concocted by the two members of the Triple Alliance, Germany and Austria. But the third member of that Alliance, Italy, found it to be an act of aggression on their part which brought on the war, and that the terms of the Triple Alliance, therefore, did not bind her to take any part.

The peace parleys which passed between the several nations involved are carefully reviewed by Mr. Beck, who concludes, as we think justly, that up to the 28th of July, when the German Imperial Chancellor sent for the English Ambassador and announced the refusal of his Government to accept the conference of the Powers proposed by Sir Edward Grey, every proposal to preserve peace had come from the Triple Entente, and that every such proposal had met with an uncompromising negative from Austria, and either that or obstructive quibbles from Germany.

At this point, the sudden return of the Kaiser to Berlin from his annual holiday in Norway, which his own Foreign Office regretted as a step taken on his Majesty's own initiative and which they feared might cause speculation and excitement, and his personal intervention from that time until his troops invaded Luxemburg and he made his abrupt demand upon the Belgian Government for permission to cross its territory are reviewed with great force and effect by Mr. Beck, with the conclusion on his part that the Kaiser, who by a timely word to Austria might have prevented all the terrible trouble that followed, was the supremely guilty party, and that such will be the verdict of history.

Mr. Beck's review of the case of Belgium is extremely interesting, and his conclusion that England, France, Russia, and Belgium can await with confidence the world's final verdict that their quarrel was just, rests safely upon the plea of "Guilty" by Germany, a conclusion which seems to have been already plainly declared by most of the civilized nations of the world.

We think that Mr. Beck's opinion that England and France were taken unawares and were wholly unprepared for war is a little too strongly expressed. France, certainly, had been making ready for war with Germany ever since the great conflict of 1870 had resulted in her loss of Alsace and Lorraine, and had had a fixed and unalterable determination to get them back when she could, although It Is evident that she did not expect her opportunity to come just when and as it did. That Great Britain had no present expectation of immediate war with Germany is clearly obvious. That she had long been apprehending the danger of it in the indefinite future is very clear, but that Sir Edward Grey and the Government and the people that he represented did all that they possibly could to prevent the war seems to be clearly established.

Mr. Beck's book is so extremely interesting from beginning to end that it is difficult when once begun to lay it down and break off the reading, and we shall not be surprised to hear, not only that it has had an immense sale in England and America, but that its translation into the languages of the other nations of Europe has been demanded.

JOSEPH H. CHOATE.

NEW YORK, January 10, 1915.

FOREWORD

On the eve of the Great War I sat one evening in the reading room of the Hotel Erbprinz in classic Weimar. I had spent ten happy days in Thuringia, and had visited with deep interest a little village near Erfurt, where one of my forbears was born. I had seen Jena, from whose historic university this paternal ancestor had gone as a missionary to North America in the middle of the eighteenth century. This simple-minded German pietist had cherished the apparent delusion that even the uncivilized Indians of the American wilderness might be taught--the Bernhardis and Treitschkes to the contrary notwithstanding--that to increase the political power of a nation by the deliberate and highly systematized destruction of its neighbors was not the truest political ideal, even of an Indian tribe.

This missionary had gone most fittingly to the Commonwealth of Pennsylvania, where its enlightened founder had already given a demonstration of the truth that a treaty of peace, even though not formally expressed in a "scrap of paper," might be kept by white men and so-called savages with scrupulous fidelity for at least three quarters of a century, for even the cynical Voltaire said in sincerest admiration that the compact between William Penn and the Indians was the only treaty which was never reduced to parchment, nor ratified by an oath and yet was never broken.

When Penn, the great apostle of peace, died in England, a disappointed, ruined, and heart-broken man, and the news reached the Indians in their wigwams along the banks of the Delaware, they had for him, whom they called the "white Truth Teller" so deep a sense of gratitude that they sent to his widow a sympathetic gift of valuable skins, in memory of the "man of unbroken friendship and inviolate treaties."

These reflections in a time of broken friendships and violated treaties are not calculated to fill the man of the twentieth century with any justifiable pride.

My mind, however, as I spent the quiet evening in the historic inn of Thackeray's Pumpernickel, did not revert to these far distant associations but was full of other thoughts suggested by the most interesting section of Germany, through which it had been my privilege to pass.

I had visited Eisenach and reverentially stood within the room where the great master of music, John Sebastian Bach, had first seen the light of day, and as I saw the walls that he loved and which are forever hallowed because they once sheltered this divine genius, the question occurred to me whether he may not have done more for Germany with his immortal harmonies, which are the foundation of all modern music, than all the Treitschkes, and Bernhardis, with their gospel of racial hatred, pseudo-patriotism, and imperial aggrandizement.

I had climbed the slopes of the Wartburg and from Luther's room had gazed with delight upon the lovely Thuringian forests. Quite apart from any ecclesiastical considerations that room seemed to suggest historic Germany in its best estate. It recalled that scene of undying interest at the Diet of Worms, when the peaceful adherence to an ideal was shown to be mightier than the power of the greatest empire since the fall of Rome. The monk of Wittenburg, standing alone in the presence of the great Emperor, Charles the Fifth, and the representatives of the most powerful religious organization that the world has ever known, with his simple, "Hier stehe ich; ich kann nicht anders," represented the truest soul and highest ideal of the nobler Germany.

These and other glorious memories, suggested by Eisenach, Frankfort, Erfurt, Weimar, Jena, and Leipzig, made this pilgrimage of intense interest, and almost the only discord was the sight of the Leipzig Voelkerschlacht Denkmal, probably the largest, and certainly the ugliest monument in all the world. It has but one justification, in that it commemorates war, and no monument ever more fully symbolized by its own colossal crudity the moral ugliness of that most ghastly phenomenon of human life. Let us pray that in the event of final victory Prussia will not commission the architects of the Leipzig monument, or the imperial designer that rebuild that Gothic masterpiece, the Rheims Cathedral. That day in Leipzig an Alsatian cartoonist, Hansi, had been sentenced to one year's imprisonment for a harmless cartoon in a book for children, in which the most supersensitive should have found occasion for nothing, except a passing smile.

On the library table of the Erbprinz, I found a large book, which proved to be a Bismarck memorial volume. It contained hundreds of pictures glorifying and almost deifying the Iron Chancellor. One particularly arrested my attention. It was the familiar picture of the negotiations for peace between Bismarck and Jules Favre in the terrible winter of 1871. The French statesman has sunk into a chair in abject despair, struck speechless by the demands of the conqueror. Bismarck stands triumphant and his proud bearing and arrogant manner fail to suggest any such magnanimous courtesy as that with which Grant accepted the sword of Lee at Appomattox. The picture breathed the very spirit of "v?victis." Had a French artist painted this picture, I could understand it, for it would serve effectively to stimulate undying hatred in the French heart. It seemed strange that a German artist should treat a subject, calling for a spirit of most delicate courtesy, in a manner which represented Prussian militarism in its most arrogant form.

This unworthy picture reminded me of a later scene in the Reichstag, in which the Iron Chancellor, after reviewing with complacency the profitable results of Germany's deliberately provoked wars against Denmark, Austria, and France, added the pious ejaculation:

Wir Deutsche fechten Gott sonst nichts in der Welt. (We Germans fear God but nothing else in the world.)

It is not necessary to impeach the sincerity of this pious glorification of the successful results of land grabbing. The mind in moments of exaltation plays strange tricks with the soul. Bismarck may have dissembled on occasion but he was never a hypocrite. It is the spirit which inspired this boastful and arrogant speech, which has so powerfully stimulated Prussian Junkerism, to which I wish to refer.

Had an American uttered these words we would have treated the boast as a vulgar exhibition of provincial "spread-eagleism," such as characterized certain classes in this country before the Civil War, and which Charles Dickens somewhat over-caricatured in Martin Chuzzlewit, but in the mouth of Bismarck, with his cynical indifference to moral considerations in questions of statecraft, this piece of rhetorical spread double-eagleism, manifests the spirit of the Prussian military caste since its too easy triumph over France in 1870-1871, a triumph, which may yet prove the greatest calamity that ever befell Germany, not only in the seeds of hatred which it sowed, of which there is now a harvest of blood past precedent, but also in the development of an arrogant pride which has profoundly affected to its prejudice the noble Germany of Luther, Bach, Beethoven, Goethe, Schiller, Kant, Humboldt, and Lessing.

To say that Germany "fears" nothing save God is contradicted by its whole diplomatic history of the last half century. In this it is not peculiar. The curse of modern statecraft is the largely unreasoning fear which all nations have of their neighbors. England has feared Germany only less than Germany has feared England and this nervous apprehension has bred jealousy, hatred, suspicion, until to-day all civilized nations are reaping a harvest horrible beyond expression.

The whole history of Germany since 1870 has shown a constant, and at times an unreasoning fear, first of France, then of the Slav, and latterly and in its most acute form, of England. I do not mean that Germany has been or is now animated by any spirit of craven cowardice. There has not been in recorded history a braver nation, and the dauntless courage with which, even at this hour, thousands of Germans are going with patriotic songs on their lips to "their graves as to their beds," is worthy of all admiration.

The whole statecraft of Germany for over forty years has been inspired by an exaggerated apprehension of the intentions of its great neighbors. This fear followed swiftly upon the triumph of 1871, for Germany early showed its apprehension that France might recover its military strength. When that fallen but indomitable foe again struggled to its feet in 1875, the Prussian military caste planned to give the stricken gladiator the coup de gr鈉e and was only prevented by the intervention of England and Russia. Later this acute and neurotic apprehension took the form of a hatred and fear of Russia, and this notwithstanding the fact that the Kaiser had in the Russo-Japanese War exalted the Czar as the "champion of Christianity" and the "representative of the white race" in the Far East.

When the psychology of the present conflict is considered by future historians, this neuropathic feature of Germany's foreign policy will be regarded as a contributing element of first importance.

Latterly the Furor Teutonicus was especially directed against England, and although it was obvious to the dispassionate observer in neutral countries that no nation was making less preparations or was in point of fact so illy prepared for a conflict as England, nevertheless Germany, with a completeness of preparation such as the world has never witnessed, was constantly indulging in a very hysteria of fear at the imaginary designs of England upon Germany's standing as a world power.

Luther's famous saying, already quoted, and Bismarck's blustering speech to the Reichstag measure the difference between the Germany of the Reformation and the Prussia of to-day.

I refuse to believe that this Bismarckian attitude is that of the German people. If a censored press permitted them to know the real truth with respect to the present crisis, that people, still sound in heart and steadfast in soul, would repudiate a policy of duplicity, cunning, and arrogance, which has precipitated their great nation into an abyss of disaster. The normal German is an admirable citizen, quiet, peaceable, thrifty, industrious, faithful, efficient, and affectionate to the verge of sentimentality. He, and not the Junker, has made Germany the most efficient political State in the world. If to his genius for organization could be added the individualism of the American, the resultant product would be incomparable. A combination of the German fortiter in re with the American suaviter in modo would make the most efficient republic in the world.

The Germany of Luther, that still survives and will survive when "Junkerism" is a dismal memory of the past, believes that "the supreme wisdom, the paramount vitality, is an abiding honesty, the doing of right, because right is right, in scorn of consequence."

That the German people have rallied with enthusiastic unanimity to the flag in this great crisis, I do not question. This is, in part, due to the fact that the truth has never yet been disclosed to them, and is not likely to be until the war is over. They have been taught that in a time of profound peace England, France, and Russia deliberately initiated a war of aggression to destroy the commercial power of Germany. The documents hereinafter analyzed will show how utterly baseless this fiction is. Even if the truth were known, no one can blame the German, who now rallies to his flag with such superhuman devotion, for whether the cause of his country is just or unjust, its prestige, and perhaps its very existence, is at stake, and there should be for the rank and file of the German people only a feeling of profound pity and deep admiration. Edmund Burke once said, "We must pardon something to the spirit of liberty." We can paraphrase it and say in this crisis, "We must pardon something to the spirit of patriotism." The whole-hearted devotion of this great nation to its flag is worthy of the best traditions of the Teutonic race. Thor did not wield his thunder hammer with greater effect than these descendants of the race of Wotan. If the ethical question depended upon relative bravery, who could decide between the German, "faithful unto death"; the English soldier, standing like a stone wall against fearful odds, the French or Russian not less brave or resolute, and the Belgian, now as in Caesar's time the "bravest of all the tribes of Gaul."

No consideration, either of sympathy, admiration, or pity, can in any manner affect the determination of the great ethical question as to the moral responsibility for the present crime against civilization. That must be determined by the facts as they have been developed, and the nations and individuals who are responsible for this world-wide catastrophe must be held to a strict accountability. The truth of history inexorably demands this.

To determine where this moral responsibility lies is the purpose of these pages.

In determining this question Posterity will distinguish between the military caste, headed by the Kaiser and the Crown Prince, which precipitated this great calamity, and the German people.

The very secrecy of the plot against the peace of the world and the failure to disclose to the German nation the diplomatic communications hereinafter quoted, strongly suggest that this detestable war is not merely a crime against civilization, but also against the deceived and misled German people. They have a vision and are essentially progressive and peace-loving in their national characteristics, while the ideals of their military caste are those of the dark ages.

One day the German people will know the full truth and then there will be a dreadful reckoning for those who have plunged a noble nation into this unfathomable gulf of suffering.

Though the mills of God grind slowly, Yet they grind exceeding small, Though with patience He stands waiting, With exactness grinds He all.

JAMES M. BECK.

NEW YORK, November 30, 1914.

The Witnesses

ENGLAND

HIS MAJESTY, KING GEORGE V.

MR. ASQUITH Premier. MR. BEAUMONT Councilor of Embassy at Constantinople. SIR F. BERTIE Ambassador at Paris. SIR G. BUCHANAN Ambassador at St. Petersburg. SIR M. DE BUNSEN Ambassador at Vienna. SIR E. GOSCHEN Ambassador at Berlin. SIR EDWARD GREY Foreign Secretary. SIR A. JOHNSTONE Minister at Luxemburg. SIR ARTHUR NICHOLSON Under Secretary for Foreign Affairs. SIR R. RODD Ambassador to Italy. SIR H. RUMBOLD Councilor of Embassy at Berlin. SIR F. VILLIERS Minister to Belgium.

GERMANY

HIS MAJESTY, EMPEROR WILLIAM II.

HERR VON BELOW (SALESKE[2]) Minister to Belgium. DR. VON BETHMANN-HOLLWEG Chancellor. HERR VON BUCH Minister at Luxemburg. HERR VON HEERINGEN Minister of War. HERR VON JAGOW Secretary of State. PRINCE LICHNOWSKY Ambassador at London. HERR VON MUELLER Minister at The Hague. COUNT POURTALES Ambassador at St. Petersburg. BARON VON SCHOEN Ambassador at Paris. HERR VON ZIMMERMANN Under Secretary of State. HERR VON TSCHIRSCHKY Ambassador at Vienna.

[Footnote 2: Herr von Below Saleske is referred to in despatches as Herr von Below.]

FRANCE

PRESIDENT RAYMOND POINCAR?
M. VIVIANI Premier of France. M. BERTHELOT Of the French Ministry for Foreign Affairs. M. PAUL CAMBON Ambassador to England. M. KLOBUKOWSKI Minister to Belgium. M. DE MARGERIE Of the French Diplomatic Service. M. JULES CAMBON Ambassador to Germany.

RUSSIA

HIS MAJESTY, EMPEROR NICHOLAS II.

M. SAZONOF Minister of Foreign Affairs. COUNT BENCKENDORFF Ambassador at London. M. BRONFWSKY Charg?d'Affaires at Berlin. M. DE ETTER Councilor of Embassy at London. M. ISVOLSKY Ambassador to France. PRINCE KUDACHEF Councilor of Embassy at Vienna. M. SALVIATI Consul General at Fiume. M. SCHEBEKO Ambassador to Austria. M. SEVASTOPOULO Charg?d'Affaires at Paris. M. STRANDTMAN Charg?d'Affaires at Belgrade. M. SUCHOMLINOF Minister for War. M. DE SWERBEEW Ambassador to Germany.

BELGIUM

HIS MAJESTY, KING ALBERT

M. DAVIGNON Minister of Foreign Affairs. BARON VON DER ELST Secretary General to Ministry of Foreign Affairs. COUNT ERREMBAULT DE DUDZEELE

Minister at Vienna. BARON FALLON Minister at The Hague. BARON GRENIER Minister at Madrid. BARON GUILLAUME Minister at Paris. COUNT DE LALAING Minister at London.

SERVIA

HIS MAJESTY, KING PETER

M. PACHITCH Premier and Minister of Foreign Affairs. M. BOSCHKOVITCH Minister at London. DR. PATCHOU Minister of Finance.

AUSTRIA

HIS MAJESTY, EMPEROR FRANCIS JOSEPH

COUNT BERCHTOLD Minister of Foreign Affairs. COUNT CLARY UND ALDRINGEN Minister at Brussels. BARON GIESL VON GIESLINGEN Minister at Belgrade. BARON MACCHIO Councilor of Austrian Ministry of Foreign Affairs. COUNT MENSDORFF Ambassador to England. COUNT SZ 罰罵 Y Ambassador to Russia.

ITALY

HIS MAJESTY, KING VICTOR EMMANUEL III.

MARQUIS DI SAN GIULIANO Minister of Foreign Affairs.

CONTENTS

THE SUPREME COURT OF CIVILIZATION

Existence of the Court--The conscience of mankind--The philosophy of Bernhardi--The recrudescence of Machiavelliism--Treitschke and Bernhardi's doctrine--Recent utterances of the Kaiser, Crown Prince, and representative officials--George Bernard Shaw's defense--Concrete illustration of Bernhardiism

CHAPTER II

THE RECORD IN THE CASE

The issues stated--Proximate and underlying causes--A war of diplomats--The masses not parties to the war--The official defenses--The English White Paper--The German White Paper--The Russian Orange Paper--The Belgian Gray Paper--Austria and Italy still silent--Obligation of these nations to disclose facts

CHAPTER III

THE SUPPRESSED EVIDENCE

No apparent suppression by England, Russia, and Belgium--Suppression by Germany of vital documents--Suppression by Austria of entire record--Significance of such suppression

CHAPTER IV

GERMANY'S RESPONSIBILITY FOR THE AUSTRIAN ULTIMATUM

Silence which preceded ultimatum--Europe's ignorance of impending developments--Duty to civilization--Germany's prior knowledge of ultimatum--Its disclaimer to Russia, France, and England of any responsibility--Contradictory admission in its official defense--Further confirmation in Germany's simultaneous threat to the Powers--Further confirmation in its confidential notice to States of Germany to prepare for eventualities

CHAPTER V

THE AUSTRIAN ULTIMATUM TO SERVIA

Extreme brutality of ultimatum--Limited time given to Servia and Europe for consideration--Ultimatum and Servia's reply contrasted in parallel columns--Relative size of two nations--Germany's intimations to Servia--Brutality of ultimatum shown by analogy--Disclaimer of intention to take territory valueless

CHAPTER VI

THE PEACE PARLEYS

Possibility of peace not embarrassed by popular clamor--Difficulties of peaceful solution not insuperable--Policy of Germany and Austria--Russia's and England's request for time--Germany's refusal to cooperate--Germany's and Austria's excuses for refusal to give extension of time--Berchtold's absence from Vienna--Austria's alleged disclaimer of territorial expansion--Sazonof's conference with English and French Ambassadors--Their conciliatory counsel to Servia--Servia's pacific reply to ultimatum--Austria, without considering Servian reply, declares war--England proposes suspension of hostilities for peace parleys--Germany refuses--Its specious reasons--Germany's untenable position as to localization of conflict--England's proposal for a conference--Germany's refusal--Austria declines all intervention, refusing to discuss Servian note--Germany supports her with a quibble as to name of conference--Russia proposes further discussion on basis of Servian note--Russia then again proposes European conference--Austria and Germany decline
CHAPTER VII

THE ATTITUDE OF FRANCE

The French Yellow Book--Its editors and contents--M. Jules Cambon--The weakness of German diplomacy--Cambon's experience and merits--Interview between the German Kaiser and the King of Belgium--The Kaiser's change of attitude--The influence of the Moroccan crisis--The condition of the German people in 1913--The suppression of news in Austria--Attitude of the military party--Servia's warning to Austria--Germany's knowledge of the Austrian ultimatum before its issuance--Italy's ignorance of the Austrian ultimatum--Significance of the fact--Germany's reasons for concealing its intentions from Italy--The policy of secrecy--Prince Lichnowsky's anxiety--Cambon's interview with von Jagow--The methods of deception--Sazonof's frank offer--Germany's attempt to influence France--Cambon's dramatic interview with von Jagow--His plea "In the name of humanity"--The different attitudes of the two groups of powers

CHAPTER VIII

THE INTERVENTION OF THE KAISER

The Kaiser's return to Berlin--His inconsistent record and complex personality--German Foreign Office deprecates his return--Its many blunders--The Kaiser takes the helm--He telegraphs the Czar--The Czar's reply--The Kaiser's second telegram--His untenable position--The Czar's explanation of military preparations and pledge that no provocative action would be taken by Russia--King George's telegram proposing temporary occupation by Austria of Belgrade pending further peace negotiations--The Kaiser's reply--The Kaiser's telegram to the Czar demanding Russian discontinuance of military preparations--His insistence upon unilateral conditions--Germany's preparations for war--Its offer to England to insure its neutrality--England's reply--Russia's offer to stop conditionally military preparations--England requests Germany to suggest any peace formula--Austria expresses willingness to discuss with Russia Servian note--Motives of Austria for this reversal of policy--The Kaiser sends ultimatum to Russia--The Czar's last appeal--The Kaiser's reply--Russia's inability to recall mobilization--England's last efforts for peace--Germany declares war--The Czar's telegram to King George

CHAPTER IX

THE CASE OF BELGIUM

The verdict of history not affected by result of war--Belgium at outbreak of war--The Treaty of 1839--Its affirmation by Bismarck--France's action in 1871--Reaffirmation by Germany of Belgian neutrality in 1911-1914--The Hague

CHAPTER X

THE JUDGMENT OF THE WORLD

EPILOGUE

The Evidence in the Case

CHAPTER I

THE SUPREME COURT OF CIVILIZATION

Let us suppose that in this year of dis-Grace, 1914, there had existed, as let us pray will one day exist, a Supreme Court of Civilization, before which the sovereign nations could litigate their differences without resort to the iniquitous arbitrament of arms and that each of the contending nations had a sufficient leaven of Christianity or shall we say commonplace, everyday morality, to have its grievances adjudged not by the ethics of the cannon, but by the eternal criterion of justice.

What would be the judgment of that august tribunal?

It may be suggested that the question is academic, as no such Supreme Court exists or is likely to exist within the life of any living man.

Casuists of the Bernhardi school of moral philosophy will further suggest that to discuss the ethical merits of the war is to start with a false premise that such a thing as international morality exists, and that when once the conventionalities of civilization are laid aside the leading nations commence and make war in a manner that differs only in degree and not in kind from the methods of Frederick the Great and Napoleon, and that these in turn only differed in degree from those of Alaric and Attila. According to this theory, the only law of nations is that ascribed by the poet to Rob Roy:

"The good old rule Sufficeth them, the simple plan That they should take who have the power, And they should keep who can."

Does the Twentieth Century only differ from its predecessors in having a thin veneering of hypocrisy, or has there developed in the progress of civilization an international morality, by which, even though imperfectly, the moral conduct of nations is judged?

The answer can be an unqualified affirmative. With the age of the printing press, the steamship, the railroad, and the telegraph there has developed a conscience of mankind.

When the founders of the American Republic severed the tie which bound them to Great Britain, they stated that "a decent respect to the opinions of mankind requires that they should declare the causes which impel them to the separation."

The Declaration assumed that there was a rule of right and wrong that regulated the intercourse of nations as well as individuals; it believed that there was a great human conscience, which rises higher than the selfish interests and prejudices of nations and races, and which approves justice and condemns injustice. It felt that this approval is more to be desired than national advantage. It constituted mankind a judge between contending nations and lest its judgment should temporarily err it established posterity as a court of last resort. It placed the tie of humanity above that of nationality. It proclaimed the solidarity of mankind.

In the years that have intervened since this noble Declaration, the world has so far progressed towards an enlightened sense of justice that a "decent respect to the opinions of mankind" has proved an efficient power in regulating peacefully and justly the intercourse of nations. Each nation does at least in some measure fear to-day the disapproval of civilization. The time gives this proof in the eager desire of Germany to-day--despite its policy of "blood and iron"--to gain the sympathetic approval of the American people, not with the remotest hope of any practical cooperation but to avoid that state of moral isolation, in which the land of Luther now finds itself.

The Supreme Court of Civilization does exist. It consists of cosmopolitan men in every country, who put aside racial and national prejudices and determine the right and wrong of every issue between nations by that slowly forming system of international morality which is the conscience of mankind.

To a certain class of German statesmen and philosophers this Court of Public Opinion is a visionary abstraction. A group of distinguished German soldiers, professors, statesmen, and even doctors of divinity, pretending to speak in behalf of the German nation, have consciously or unconsciously attempted to revive in the twentieth century the cynical political morality of the sixteenth.

As Symonds, the historian of the Renaissance, says in his Age of the Despots, Machiavelli was the first in modern times to formulate a theory of government in which the interests of the ruler are alone regarded, which assumes

a separation between statecraft and morality, which recognizes force and fraud among the legitimate means of attaining high political ends, which makes success alone the test of conduct and which presupposes the corruption, baseness, and venality of mankind at large.

Even the age of Cesare Borgia revolted against this philosophy and the name of Machiavelli became a byword. "Am I a Machiavel?" says the host in The

Merry Wives of Windsor, and the implication of this question indirectly manifests the revolt of the seventeenth century against the sinister philosophy of the great Florentine.

Nothing can be more amazing than that not only leading militarists of Germany but many of its foremost philosophers and teachers have become so intoxicated with the dream of Pan-Germanism that in the utmost sincerity they have espoused and with a certain pride proclaimed the vicious principles of Machiavelli in all their moral nudity. There is an emotional and mystical element in the advanced German thinker, which makes him capable of accepting in full sincerity intellectual and moral absurdities of which the more robust common sense of other nations would be incapable. The advanced German doctrinaire is the "wisest fool in Christendom." The depth of his learning is generally in the inverse ratio to the shallowness of his common sense.

Nothing better demonstrates this than the present negation by advanced and doubtless sincere German thinkers of the very foundations of public morality and indeed of civilization. They have been led with Nietzsche to revile the Beatitudes and exalt the supremacy of cruelty over mercy. Indeed Treitschke in his lectures on Politik, which have become the gospel of Junkerdom, avowedly based his gospel of force upon the teaching of Machiavelli, for he points out that it was Machiavelli who first clearly saw that the State is power (der Staat ist Macht). Therefore "to care for this power is the highest moral duty of the State" and "of all political weaknesses that of feebleness is the most abominable and despicable; it is the sin against the holy spirit of politics." He therefore holds that the State as the ultimate good "cannot bind its will for the future over against other States," and that international treaties are therefore only obligatory "for such time as the State may find to be convenient."

To enforce the will of the nation contrary to its own solemn promises and to increase its might, war is the appointed means. Both Treitschke and Moltke conceived it as "an ordinance set by God" and "one of the two highest functions" of the State. The doctrine is carried to the blasphemous conclusion that war is an ordinance of a just and merciful God; that, to quote Bernhardi, "it is a biological necessity" and that "the living God will see to it that war shall always recur as a terrible medicine for humanity." Therefore "might is at once the supreme right and the dispute as to what is right is decided by the arbitrament of war," which gives a "biologically just decision."

This means that the 42 centimeter howitzer is more moral than a gun of smaller caliber and that the justice of God depends upon the superiority of Krupp to other ordnance manufacturers.

Treitschke tells us, and the statement is quoted by Bernhardi with approval, that "the end all and be all of a state is power, and he who is not man enough to look this truth in the face should not meddle with politics." To this Bernhardi adds that the State's highest moral duty is to increase its power and in so doing "the State is the sole judge of the morality of its own action. It is in fact above morality or, in other words whatever is necessary is moral."

Again we learn that the State must not allow any conventional sympathies to distract it from its object and that "conditions may arise which are more powerful than the most honorable intentions."

All efforts directed towards the abolition of war are denominated as not only "foolish but absolutely immoral." To indicate that in this prosecution of war for the increase of dominion, chivalry would be a weakness and magnanimity a crime, we are finally told that "the State is a law unto itself" and that "weak nations have not the same right to live as powerful and vigorous nations." Even as to weak nations, we are further advised that the powerful and vigorous nation--which alone apparently has the right to live-- must not wait for some act of aggression or legitimate casus belli, but that it is justified in deliberately provoking a war, and that the happiest results have always followed such "deliberately provoked wars," for "the prospects of success are the greatest when the moment for declaring war can be selected to suit the political and military situation."

As the weak nations have no moral right to live it becomes important to remember that in the economy of Prussian Junkerdom there is only one strong race--his own. "Wir sind die Weltrasse." The ultimate goal is the super-nation, and the premise upon which the whole policy is based is that Germany is predestined to be that super-nation. Bernhardi believes--and his belief is but the reflex of the oft-repeated boast of the Kaiser--that history presents no other possibility. "For us there are two alternatives and no third--

world power or ruin" (Weltmacht oder Niedergang). To assimilate Germany to ancient Rome the Kaiser on occasion reminds himself of Caesar and affects to reign, not by the will of the people, but by divine right. No living monarch has said or done more to revive this medi 鐶 al fetich. To his soldiers he has recently said: "You think each day of your Emperor. Do not forget God." What magnanimity!

At the outbreak of the present war he again illustrated his spirit of fanatical absolutism, which at times inspires him, by saying to his army:

Remember that the German people are the chosen of God. On me, as German Emperor, the spirit of God has descended. I am His weapon; His sword; His Vicegerent. Woe to the disobedient! Death to cowards and unbelievers!

The modern world has had nothing like this since Mahomet and, accepted literally, it claims for the Kaiser the divine attributes attributed to the Caesars. Even the Caesars, in baser and more primitive times, found posing as a divine superman somewhat difficult and disconcerting. Shakespeare subtly suggests this when he makes his Caesar talk like a god and act with the vacillation of a child.

When the war was precipitated as the natural result of such abhorrent teachings, the world at large knew little either of Treitschke or Bernhardi. Thoughtful men of other nations did know that the successful political immoralities of Frederick the Great had profoundly affected the policies of the Prussian Court to this day. The German poet, Freiligrath, once said that "Germany is Hamlet," but no analogy is less justified. There is nothing in the supersensitive, introspective, and amiable dreamer of Elsinore to suggest the Prussia of to-day, which Bebel has called "Siegesbetrunken." (Victory-drunk.)

Since the beginning of the present war, the world has become familiar with these abhorrent teachings and as a result of a general revolt against this recrudescence of Borgiaism attempts have been made by the apologists for Prussia, especially in the United States, to suggest that neither Treitschke nor Bernhardi fairly reflect the political philosophy of official Germany. Treitschke's influence as an historian and lecturer could not well be denied but attempts have been made to impress America that Bernhardi has no standing to speak for his country and that the importance of his teachings should therefore be minimized.

Apart from the wide popularity of Bernhardi's writings in Germany, the German Government has never repudiated Bernhardi's conclusions or disclaimed responsibility therefor. While possibly not an officially authorized spokesman, yet he is as truly a representative thinker in the German military system as Admiral Mahan was in the Navy of the United States. Of the acceptance by Prussia of Bernhardi's teachings there is one irrefutable proof. It is Belgium. The destruction of that unoffending country is the full harvest of this twentieth-century Machiavelliism.

A few recent utterances from a representative physician, a prominent journalist, and a distinguished retired officer of the German Army may be quoted as showing how completely infatuated a certain class of German thinkers has become with the gospel of force for the purpose of attaining world power.

Thus a Dr. Fuchs, in a book on the subject of preparedness for war, says:

Therefore the German claim of the day must be: The family to the front. The State has to follow at first in the school, then in foreign politics. Education to hate. Education to the estimation of hatred. Organization of hatred. Education to the desire for hatred. Let us abolish unripe and false shame before brutality and fanaticism. We must not hesitate to announce: To us is given faith, hope, and hatred, but hatred is the greatest among them.

Maximilian Harden, one of the most influential German journalists, says:

Let us drop our miserable attempts to excuse Germany's action. Not against our will and as a nation taken by surprise did we hurl ourselves into this gigantic venture. We willed it. We had to will it. We do not stand before the judgment seat of Europe. We acknowledge no such jurisdiction. Our might shall create a new law in Europe. It is Germany that strikes. When she has conquered new domains for her genius then the priesthoods of all the gods will praise the God of War.

Still more striking and morally repellent was the very recent statement by

Major-General von Disfurth, in an article contributed by him to the Hamburger Nachrichten, which so completely illustrates Bernhardiism in its last extreme of avowed brutality that it justifies quotation in extenso.

No object whatever is served by taking any notice of the accusations of barbarity leveled against Germany by our foreign critics. Frankly, we are and must be barbarians, if by these we understand those who wage war relentlessly and to the uttermost degree....

We owe no explanations to any one. There is nothing for us to justify and nothing to explain away. Every act of whatever nature committed by our troops for the purpose of discouraging, defeating, and destroying our enemies is a brave act and a good deed, and is fully justified.... Germany stands as the supreme arbiter of her own methods, which in the time of war must be dictated to the world....

They call us barbarians. What of it? We scorn them and their abuse. For my part I hope that in this war we have merited the title of barbarians. Let neutral peoples and our enemies cease their empty chatter, which may well be compared to the twitter of birds. Let them cease their talk of the Cathedral at Rheims and of all the churches and all the castles in France which have shared its fate. These things do not interest us. Our troops must achieve victory. What else matters?

These hysterical vaporings of advanced Junkers no more make a case against the German people than the tailors of Tooley Street had authority to speak for England, but they do represent the spirit of the ruling caste, to which unhappily the German people have committed their destiny. It would not be difficult to quote both the Kaiser and the Crown Prince, who on more than one occasion have manifested their enthusiastic adherence to the gospel of brute force. The world is not likely to forget the Crown Prince's congratulations to the brutal military martinet of the Zabern incident, and still less the shameful fact that when the Kaiser sent his punitive expedition to China, he who once stood within sight of the Mount of Olives and preached a sermon breathing the spirit of Christian humility, said to his soldiers:

When you encounter the enemy you will defeat him. No quarter shall be given, no prisoners shall be taken. Let all who fall into your hands be at your mercy. Just as the Huns a thousand years ago under the leadership of Etzel (Attila), gained a reputation in virtue of which they still live in historical tradition, so may the name of Germany become known in such a manner in China that no Chinaman will ever again even dare to look askance at a German.

And this campaign of extermination--worthy of a savage Indian chief--was planned for the most pacific and unaggressive race, the Chinese, for it is sadly true that the one nation which has more than any other been inspired for two thousand years by the spirit of "peace on earth" is the hermit nation, into which until the nineteenth century the light of Christianity never shone.

In a recent article, George Bernard Shaw, the Voltaire of the twentieth century, with the intellectual brilliancy and moral shallowness of the great cynic, attempts to justify Bernhardiism by resort to the unconvincing "et tu quoque" argument. He contends that England also has had its "Bernhardis," and refers to a few books which he affects to think bear out his argument. That these books show that there have been advocates of militarism in England is undoubtedly true. The present war illustrates that there was need of such literature, for a nation which faced so great a trial as the present, with a standing army that was pitiful in comparison with that of Germany and without any involuntary service law, certainly had need of some literary stimulus to self-preparation. No one quarrels with Bernhardi in his discussions of the problems of war as such. It is only when the soldier ceases to be a strategist and becomes a moralist that the average man with conventional ideas of morality revolts against Bernhardiism. The books to which Mr. Shaw refers can be searched in vain for any passages parallel to those which have been quoted from Treitschke, Bernhardi, and other German writers. The brilliant but erratic George Bernard Shaw cannot find in all English literature any such Machiavelliisms as those of Treitschke and Bernhardi.

Shaw's whole defense of Germany, betrays his characteristic desire to be clever and audacious without regard to nice considerations of truth. Much as we may admire his intellectual badinage under other circumstances, it may be questioned whether in this supreme tragedy of the world it was fitting for Shaw to daub himself anew with his familiar vermilion and play the intellectual clown.

It was either courage of an extraordinary but unenviable character or else crass stupidity that led Bernhardi to submit to the civilization of the present day such a debasing gospel, for if his brain had not been hopelessly obfuscated by his Pan-Germanic imperialism, he would have seen that not only would this philosophy do his country infinitely more harm than a whole park of artillery but would inevitably carry his memory down to a wondering posterity, like Machiavelli, detestable but, unlike Machiavelli, ridiculous.

Machiavelli gave to his Prince a literary finish that placed his treatise among the classics, while Bernhardi has gained recognition chiefly because his book is a moral anachronism.

One concrete illustration from Bernhardi clearly shows that the sentences above quoted are truly representative of his philosophy, and not unfair excerpts. In explaining that it is the duty of every nation to increase its power and territory without regard for the rights of others, he alludes to the fact that England committed the "unpardonable blunder from her point of view of not supporting the Southern States in the American War of Secession," and thus forever severing in twain the American Republic. In this striking illustration of applied Bernhardiism, there is no suggestion as to the moral side of such intervention. Nothing is said with respect to the moral question of slavery, or of the obligations of England to a friendly Power. Nothing as to how the best hopes of humanity would have been shattered if the American Republic--that "pillar of cloud by day and pillar of fire by night" to struggling humanity--had been brought to cureless ruin. All these considerations are completely disregarded, and all Bernhardi can see in the situation, as it presented itself to England in 1861, was its opportunity, by a cowardly stab in the back, to remove forever from its path a great and growing nation.

Poor Bernhardi! He thought to serve his royal master. He has simply damned him. As Machiavelli, as the eulogist of the Medicis, simply emphasized their moral nudity, so Bernhardi has shown the world the inner significance of this crude revival of Caesarism.

CHAPTER II

THE RECORD IN THE CASE

All morally sane men in this twentieth century are agreed that war abstractly is an evil thing,--perhaps the greatest of all indecencies,--and that while it may be one of the offenses which must come, "woe to that man (or nation) by whom the offense cometh!"

They are of one mind in regarding this present war as a great crime--perhaps the greatest crime--against civilization, and the only questions which invite discussion are:

Which of the two contending groups of Powers is morally responsible?

Was Austria justified in declaring war against Servia?

Was Germany justified in declaring war against Russia and France?

Was Germany justified in declaring war against Belgium?

Was England justified in declaring war against Germany?

Primarily and perhaps exclusively these ethical questions turn upon the issues developed by the communications which passed between the various chancelleries of Europe in the last week of July, for it is the amazing feature of this greatest of wars that it was precipitated by the ruling classes and, assuming that all the diplomats sincerely desired a peaceful solution of the questions raised by the Austrian ultimatum (which is by no means clear) the war is the result of ineffective diplomacy.

I quite appreciate the distinction between the immediate causes of a war and the anterior or underlying causes. The fundamental cause of the Franco-German War of 1870 was not the incident at Ems nor even the question of the Spanish succession. These were but the precipitating pretexts or, as a lawyer would express it, the "proximate causes." The underlying cause was unquestionably the rivalry between Prussia and France for political supremacy in Europe.

Behind the Austrian ultimatum to Servia were also great questions of State policy, not easily determinable upon any tangible ethical principle, and which involved the hegemony of Europe. Germany's domination of Europe had been established when by the rattling of its saber it compelled Russia in 1908 to permit Austria to disturb the then existing status in the Balkans by the forcible annexation of Bosnia and Herzegovina, and behind the Austrian-Servian question of 1914, arising out of the murder of the Crown Prince of Austria at Serajevo, was the determination of Germany and Austria to reassert that dominant position by compelling Russia to submit to a further humiliation of a Slav State.

The present problem is to inquire how far Germany and her ally selected a just pretext to test this question of mastery.

The pretext was the work of diplomatists. It was not the case of a nation rising upon some great cause which appealed to popular imagination. The acts of the statesmen in that last fateful week of July, 1914, were not the mere echo of the popular will.

The issues were framed by the statesmen and diplomats of Europe and whatever efforts were made to preserve the peace and whatever obstructive tactics were interposed were not the acts of any of the nations now in arms but those of a small coterie of men who, in the secrecy of their respective cabinets, made their moves and countermoves upon the chessboard of nations.

The future of Europe in that last week of July was in the hands of a small group of men, numbering not over fifty, and what they did was never known to their respective nations in any detail until after the fell Rubicon had been crossed and a world war had been precipitated.

If all of these men had sincerely desired to work for peace, there would not have been any war.

So swiftly did events move that the masses of the people had time neither to think nor to act. The suddenness of the crisis marks it as a species of "mid-summer madness," a very "witches' sabbath" of diplomatic demagoguery.

In a peaceful summer, when the nations now struggling to exterminate each other were fraternizing in the holiday centers of Europe, an issue was suddenly precipitated, made the subject of communications between the various chancelleries, and almost in the twinkling of an eye Europe found itself wrapped in a universal flame. The appalling toll of death suggests the inquiry of Hamlet: "Did these bones cost no more the breeding, but to play at loggats with 'em?" and if the diplomatic "loggats" of 1914 were ineffectively played, some one must accept the responsibility for such failure.

This sense of responsibility against the dread Day of Accounting has resulted in a disposition beyond past experience to justify the quarrel by placing before the world the diplomatic record.

The English Government commenced shortly after the outbreak of hostilities by publishing the so-called White Paper, consisting of a statement by the British Government and 160 diplomatic documents as an appendix. This was preceded by Sir Edward Grey's masterly speech in Parliament. That speech and all his actions in this fateful crisis may rank him in future history with the younger Pitt.

On August 4th, the German Chancellor for the first time explained to the representatives of his nation assembled in the Reichstag the causes of the war, then already commenced, and there was distributed among the members a statement of the German Foreign Office, accompanied by 27 Exhibits in the form of diplomatic communications, which have been erroneously called the German White Paper and which sets forth Germany's defense to the world.

Shortly thereafter Russia, casting aside all the traditional secrecy of Muscovite diplomacy, submitted to a candid world its acts and deeds in the form of the so-called Russian Orange Paper, with 79 appended documents, and this was followed later by the publication by Belgium of the so-called Belgian Gray Paper.

Late in November France published its Yellow Book, the most comprehensive of these diplomatic records. Of the two groups of powers, therefore, only Austria and Italy have failed to disclose their diplomatic correspondence to the scrutiny of the world.

The former, as the originator of the controversy, should give as a matter of "decent respect to the opinions of mankind" its justification, if any, for what it did. So far, it has only given its ultimatum to Servia and Servia's reply.

Italy, as a nation that has elected to remain neutral, is not under the same moral obligation to disclose the secrets of its Foreign Office, and while it remains on friendly terms with all the Powers it probably feels some delicacy in disclosing confidential communications, but as the whole world is vitally interested in determining the justice of the quarrel and as it is wholly probable that the archives of the Italian Foreign Office would throw an illuminating searchlight upon the moral issues involved, Italy, in a spirit of loyalty to civilization, should without further delay disclose the documentary evidence in its possession.

While it is to be regretted that the full diplomatic record is not made up, yet as we have the most substantial part of the record in the communications which passed in those fateful days between Berlin, St. Petersburg, Paris, and London, there is sufficient before the court to justify a judgment, especially as there is reason to believe that the documents as yet withheld would only confirm the conclusions which the record already given to the world irresistibly suggests.

Thus we can reasonably assume that the Italian documentary evidence would fairly justify the conclusion that the war was on the part of Germany and Austria a war of aggression, for Italy, by its refusal to act with its associates of the Triple Alliance, has in the most significant manner thus adjudged it.

Under the terms of the Triple Alliance, Italy had obligated itself to support Germany and Austria in any purely defensive war, and if therefore the communications, which undoubtedly passed between Vienna and Berlin on the one hand, and Rome on the other, justified the conclusion that Germany and Austria had been assailed by Russia, England, and France or either of them, then we must assume that Italy would have respected its obligation, especially as it would thus relieve Italy from any possible charge of treachery to two allies, whose support and protection it had enjoyed from the time that the Triple Alliance was first made.

When Italy decided that it was under no obligation to support its allies, it effectually affirmed the fact that they had commenced a war of aggression, and until the contrary is shown, we must therefore assume that the archives of the Foreign Office at Rome would merely confirm the conclusions hereinafter set forth as to the moral responsibility for the war.

Similarly upon considerations that are familiar to all who have had any experience in the judicial investigation of truth, it must be assumed that if Austria had in its secret archives any documentary evidence that would justify it in its pretension that it had been unjustly assailed by one or more of the Powers with which it is now at war, it would have published such documents to the world in its own exculpation. The moral responsibility for this war is too great for any nation to accept it unnecessarily. Least of all could Austria-- which on the face of the record commenced the controversy by its ultimatum to Servia--leave anything undone to acquit itself at the bar of public opinion of any responsibility for the great crime that is now drenching Europe with blood. The time is past when any nation can ignore the opinions of mankind or needlessly outrage its conscience. Germany has recognized this in publishing its defense and exhibiting a part of its documentary proof, and if its ally, Austria, continues to withhold from the knowledge of the world the documents in its possession, there can be but one conclusion as to its guilt.

Upon the record thus made up in the Supreme Court of Civilization, that tribunal need no more hesitate to proceed to judgment than would an ordinary court hesitate to enter a decree because one of the litigants has deliberately suppressed documents known to be in its possession. It does not lie in the mouth of such a litigant to ask the court to suspend judgment or withhold its sentence until the full record is made up, when the incompleteness of that record is due to its own deliberate suppression of vital documentary proofs.

CHAPTER III

THE SUPPRESSED EVIDENCE

The official defenses of England, Russia, France, and Belgium do not apparently show any failure on the part of either to submit any essential diplomatic document in their possession. They have respectively made certain contentions as to the proposals that they made to maintain the peace of the world, and in every instance have supported these contentions by putting into evidence the letters and communications in which such proposals were expressed.

When the German White Paper is examined it discloses on its very face the suppression of documents of vital importance. The fact that communications passed between Berlin and Vienna, the text of which has never been disclosed, is not a matter of conjecture. Germany asserts as part of its defense that it faithfully exercised its mediatory influence on Austria, but not only is such influence not disclosed by any practical results, such as we would expect in view of her dominating relations with Austria, but the text of these vital communications is still kept in the secret archives of Berlin and Vienna. Germany has carefully selected a part of her diplomatic records for publication but withheld others. Austria has withheld all.

Thus in the official apology for Germany it is stated that, in spite of the refusal of Austria to accept the proposition of Sir Edward Grey to treat the Servian reply "as a basis for further conversations,"

we [Germany] continued our mediatory efforts to the utmost and advised Vienna to make any possible compromise consistent with the dignity of the Monarchy.[3]

[Footnote 3: German White Paper.]

This would be more convincing if the German Foreign Office had added the text of the advice which it thus gave Vienna.

A like significant omission will be found when the same official defense states that on July 29th the German Government advised Austria "to begin the conversations with Mr. Sazonof." But here again the text is not found among the documents which the German Foreign Office has given to the world. The communications, which passed between that office and its ambassadors in St. Petersburg, Paris, and London, are given in extenso, but among the twenty-seven communications appended to the German White Paper it is most significant that not a single communication is given of the many which passed from the Foreign Office of Berlin to that of Vienna and only two which passed from the German Ambassador in Vienna to the

German Chancellor. While the Kaiser has favored the world with his messages to the Czar and King George, he has wholly failed to give us any message that he sent in those critical days to the Austrian Emperor or the King of Italy. We shall have occasion to refer hereafter to the frequent failure to produce documents, the existence of which is admitted by the exhibits which Germany appended to its White Paper.

This cannot be an accident. The German Foreign Office has seen fit to throw the veil of secrecy over the text of its communications to Vienna, although professing to give the purport of a few of them. The purpose of this suppression is even more clearly indicated by the complete failure of Austria to submit any of its diplomatic records to the scrutiny of a candid world. Until Germany and Austria are willing to put the most important documents in their possession in evidence, they must not be surprised that the World, remembering Bismarck's garbling of the Ems dispatch, which precipitated the Franco-Prussian War, will be incredulous as to the sincerity of their pacific protestations.

ADDENDUM

The Austrian Red Book, published more than six months after the declaration of war, simply emphasizes the policy of suppression of vital documents, which we have already discussed. Of its 69 documentary exhibits, there is not one which passed directly between the Cabinets of Berlin and Vienna. The text of the communications, in which Germany claims to have exercised a mediatory and conciliatory influence with its ally, is still withheld. Not a single document is produced which was sent between July the 6th and July the 21st, the period when the great coup was secretly planned by Berlin and Vienna.

In the Red Book we find eight communications from Count Berchtold to the Austrian Ambassador at Berlin and four replies from that official, but not a letter or telegram passing between Berchtold and von Bethmann-Hollweg or between the German and Austrian Kaisers. The Austrian Red Book gives additional evidence that at the eleventh hour, and shortly before Germany issued its ultimatum to Russia, Austria did finally agree to discuss the Servian question with Russia; but the information, which Germany presumably gave to its ally of its intention to send the ultimatum to Russia, is carefully withheld.

Notwithstanding this suppression of vital documents, the diplomatic papers of Germany and Austria, now partially given to the world, disclose an unmistakable purpose, amounting to an open confession, that they intended to force their will upon Europe, even though this course involved the most stupendous war in the history of mankind.

March 1, 1915.

CHAPTER IV

GERMANY'S RESPONSIBILITY FOR THE AUSTRIAN ULTIMATUM

On June 28, 1914, the Austrian Crown Prince was murdered at Serajevo. For nearly a month thereafter there was no public statement by Austria of its intentions, with the exception of a few semi-inspired dispatches to the effect that it would act with the greatest moderation and self-restraint. A careful examination made of the files of two leading American newspapers, each having a separate news service, from June 28, 1914, to July 23, 1914, has failed to disclose a single dispatch from Vienna which gave any intimation as to the drastic action which Austria was about to take.

The French Premier, Viviani, in his speech to the French Senate, and House of Deputies, on August 4, 1914, after referring to the fact that France, Russia, and Great Britain had cooperated in advising Servia to make any reasonable concession to Austria, added:

This advice was all the more valuable in view of the fact that Austria-Hungary's demands had been inadequately foreshadowed to the governments of the Triple Entente, to whom during the three preceding weeks the Austro-Hungarian Government had repeatedly given assurance that its demands would be extremely moderate.

The movements of the leading statesmen and rulers of the Triple Entente clearly show that they, as well as the rest of the world, had been lulled into false security either by the silence of Austria, or, as Viviani avers, by its deliberate suggestion that its treatment of the Serajevo incident would be conciliatory, pacific, and moderate.

Thus, on July 20th, the Russian Ambassador, obviously anticipating no crisis, left Vienna on a fortnight's leave of absence. The President of the French Republic and its Premier were far distant from Paris. Pachitch, the Servian Premier, was absent from Belgrade, when the ultimatum was issued.

The testimony of the British Ambassador to Vienna is to the same effect. He reports to Sir Edward Grey:

The delivery at Belgrade on the 23d of July of the note to Servia was preceded by a period of absolute silence at the Ballplatz.

He proceeds to say that with the exception of the German Ambassador at Vienna (note the significance of the exception) not a single member of the Diplomatic Corps knew anything of the Austrian ultimatum and that the French Ambassador, when he visited the Austrian Foreign Office on July 23d (the day of its issuance), was not only kept in ignorance that the ultimatum had actually been issued, but was given the impression that its tone would be moderate. Even the Italian Ambassador was not taken into Count Berchtold's confidence.[4]

[Footnote 4: Dispatch from Sir M. de Bunsen to Sir Edward Grey, dated September 1, 1914.]

The Servian Government had formally disclaimed any responsibility for the assassination and had pledged itself to punish any Servian citizen implicated therein. No word came from Vienna excepting the semi-official intimations as to its moderate and conciliatory course, and after the funeral of the Archduke, the world, then enjoying its summer holiday, had almost forgotten the Serajevo incident. The whole tragic occurrence simply survived in the sympathy which all felt with Austria in its new trouble, and especially with its aged monarch, who, like King Lear, was "as full of grief as age, wretched in both." Never was it even hinted that Germany and Austria were about to apply in a time of peace a match to the powder magazine of Europe.

Can it be questioned that loyalty to the highest interests of civilization required that Germany and Austria, when they determined to make the murder of the Archduke by an irresponsible assassin the pretext for bringing up for final decision the long-standing troubles between Austria and Servia, should have given all the European nations some intimation of their intention, so that their confr鑪es in the family of nations could cooperate to adjust this trouble, as they had adjusted far more difficult questions after the close of the Balko-Turkish War?

Whatever the issue of the present conflict, it will always be to the lasting discredit of Germany and Austria that they were false to this great duty, and that they precipitated the greatest of all wars in a manner so underhanded as to suggest a trap. They knew, as no one else knew, in those quiet mid-summer days of July, that civilization was about to be suddenly and most cruelly torpedoed. The submarine was Germany and the torpedo, Austria, and the work was most effectually done.

This ignorance of the leading European statesmen (other than those of Germany and Austria) as to what was impending is strikingly shown by the first letter in the English White Paper from Sir Edward Grey to Sir H. Rumbold, dated July 20, 1914. When this letter was written it is altogether probable that Austria's arrogant and unreasonable ultimatum had already been framed and approved in Vienna and Berlin, and yet Sir Edward Grey, the Foreign Minister of a great and friendly country, had so little knowledge of Austria's policy that he

asked the German Ambassador to-day (July 20th) if he had any news of what was going on in Vienna. He replied that he had not, but Austria was certainly going to take some step.

Sir Edward Grey adds that he told the German Ambassador that he had learned that Count Berchtold, the Austrian Foreign Minister,

in speaking to the Italian Ambassador in Vienna, had deprecated the suggestion that the situation was grave, but had said that it should be cleared up.

The German Minister then replied that it would be desirable "if Russia could act as a mediator with regard to Servia," so that the first suggestion of Russia playing the part of the peacemaker came from the German Ambassador in London. Sir Edward Grey then adds that he told the German Ambassador that he assumed that the Austrian Government would not do anything until they had first disclosed to the public their case against Servia, founded presumably upon what they had discovered at the trial,

and the German Ambassador assented to this assumption.[5]

[Footnote 5: English White Paper, No. 1.]

Either the German Ambassador was then deceiving Sir Edward Grey, or the submarine torpedo was being prepared with such secrecy that even the German Ambassador in England did not know what was then in progress.

The interesting and important question here suggests itself whether Germany had knowledge of and approved in advance the Austrian ultimatum. If it did, it was guilty of duplicity, for the German Ambassador at St. Petersburg gave to the Russian Minister of Foreign Affairs an express assurance that

the German Government had no knowledge of the text of the Austrian note before it was handed in and had not exercised any influence on its contents. It is a mistake to attribute to Germany a threatening attitude.[6]

[Footnote 6: Russian Orange Paper, No. 18.]

This statement is inherently improbable. Austria was the weaker of the two allies, and it was Germany's saber that it was rattling in the face of Europe. Obviously Austria could not have proceeded to extreme measures, which it was recognized from the first would antagonize Russia, unless it had the support of Germany, and there is a probability, amounting to a moral certainty, that it would not have committed itself and Germany to the possibility of a European war without first consulting Germany.

Moreover, we have the testimony of Sir M. de Bunsen, the English Ambassador in Vienna, who advised Sir Edward Grey that he had "private information that the German Ambassador (at Vienna) knew the text of the Austrian ultimatum to Servia before it was dispatched, and telegraphed it to the German Emperor," and that the German Ambassador himself "indorses every line of it."[7] As he does not disclose the source of his "private information," this testimony would not by itself be convincing, but when we examine Germany's official defense in the German White Paper, we find that the German Foreign Office admits that it was consulted by Austria previous to the ultimatum and not only approved of Austria's course but literally gave that country a carte blanche to proceed.

[Footnote 7: English White Paper, No. 95.]

This point seems so important in determining the sincerity of Germany's attitude and pacific protestations that we quote in extenso. After referring to the previous friction between Austria and Servia, the German White Paper says:

In view of these circumstances Austria had to admit that it would not be consistent either with the dignity or self-preservation of the Monarchy to look on longer at the operations on the other side of the border without taking action. The Austro-Hungarian Government advised us of its view of the situation and asked our opinion in the matter. We were able to assure our Ally most heartily of our agreement with her view of the situation and to assure her that any action that she might consider it necessary to take in order to put an end to the movement in Servia directed against the existence of the Austro-Hungarian Monarchy would receive our approval. We were fully aware in this connection that warlike moves on the part of Austria-Hungary against Servia would bring Russia into the question and might draw us into a war In accordance with our duties as an Ally.

Sir M. de Bunsen's credible testimony is further confirmed by the fact that the British Ambassador at Berlin in his letter of July 22d, to Sir Edward Grey, states that on the preceding night (July 21st) he had met the German Secretary of State for Foreign Affairs, and an allusion was made to a possible action by Austria.

His Excellency was evidently of opinion that this step on Austria's part would have been made ere this. He insisted that the question at issue was one for settlement between Servia and Austria alone, and that there should be no interference from outside in the discussions between those two countries.

He[8] adds that while he had regarded it as inadvisable that his country should approach Austria in the matter, he had

[Footnote 8: von Jagow.]

on several occasions, in conversation with the Servian Minister, emphasized the extreme importance that Austro-Servian relations should be put on a proper footing.[9]

[Footnote 9: English White Paper, No. 2.]

Here we have the first statement of Germany's position in the matter, a position which subsequent events showed to be entirely untenable, but to which it tenaciously adhered to the very end, and which did much to precipitate the war. Forgetful of the solidarity of European civilization, and the fact that by policy and diplomatic intercourse continuing through many centuries a united European State exists, even though its organization be as yet inchoate, he took the ground that Austria should be permitted to proceed to aggressive measures against Servia without interference from any other Power, even though, as was inevitable, the humiliation of Servia would destroy the status of the Balkan States and threaten the European balance of power. The inconsistency between Germany's claim that it could give Austria a carte blanche to proceed against Servia and agree to support its action with the sword of Germany, and the other contention that neither Russia nor any European State had any right to interfere on behalf of Servia is obvious. It was the greatest blunder of Germany's many blunders in this Tragedy of Errors.

No space need be taken in convincing any reasonable man that this Austrian ultimatum to Servia was brutal in its tone and unreasonable in its demands. It would be difficult to recall a more offensive document, and its iniquity was enhanced by the short shriving time which it gave either Servia or Europe. Servia had forty-eight hours to answer whether it would compromise its sovereignty, and virtually admit its complicity in a crime which it had steadily disavowed. The other European nations had little more than a day to consider what could be done to preserve the peace of Europe before that peace was fatally compromised.[10]

[Footnote 10: English White Paper, No. 5; Russian Orange Paper, No. 3.]

Further confirmation that the German Foreign Office did have advance knowledge of at least the substance of the ultimatum is shown by the fact that on the day the ultimatum was issued the Chancellor of the German Empire instructed its Ambassadors in Paris, London, and St. Petersburg to advise the English, French, and Russian governments that

the acts as well as the demands of the Austro-Hungarian Government cannot but be looked upon as justified.[11]

[Footnote 11: German White Paper, Annex 1 B.]

How could Germany thus indorse the "demands" if it did not know the substance of the ultimatum? Is it probable that Germany would have given in a matter of the gravest importance a blanket endorsement of Austria's demands, unless the German Government had first been fully advised as to their nature?

The hour when these instructions were sent is not given, so that it does not follow that these significant instructions were necessarily prior to the service of the ultimatum at Belgrade at 6 P.M. Nevertheless, as the ultimatum did not reach the other capitals of Europe until the following day, as the diplomatic correspondence clearly shows, it seems improbable that the German Foreign Office would have issued this very carefully prepared and formal warning to the other Powers on July the 23d unless it had full knowledge not only of Austria's intention to serve the ultimatum but also of the substance thereof.

While it may be that Germany, while indorsing in blank the policy of Austria, purposely refrained from examining the text of the communication, so that it could thereafter claim that it was not responsible for Austria's action--a policy which would not lessen the discreditable character of this iniquitous conspiracy against the peace of Europe,--yet the more reasonable assumption is that the simultaneous issuance of Austria's ultimatum at Belgrade and Germany's warning to the Powers was the result of a concerted action and had a common purpose. No court or jury, reasoning along the ordinary inferences of human life, would question this conclusion.

The communication from the German Foreign Office last referred to anticipates that Servia "will refuse to comply with these demands"--why, if they were justified?--and Germany suggests to France, England, and Russia that if, as a result of such noncompliance, Austria has "recourse to military measures," that "the choice of means must be left to it."

The German Ambassadors in the three capitals were instructed

to lay particular stress on the view that the above question is one, the settlement of which devolves solely upon Austria-Hungary and Servia, and one which the Powers should earnestly strive to confine to the two countries concerned,

and the instruction added that Germany strongly desired

that the dispute be localized, since any intervention of another Power, on account of the various alliance obligations, would bring consequences impossible to measure.

This is one of the most significant documents in the whole correspondence. If the German Foreign Office were as ignorant as its Ambassador at London affected to be of the Austrian policy and ultimatum, and if Germany were not then instigating and supporting Austria in its perilous course, why should the German Chancellor have served this threatening notice upon England, France, and Russia, that Austria "must" be left free to make war upon Servia, and that any attempt to intervene in behalf of the weaker nation would "bring consequences impossible to measure"?[12]

[Footnote 12: German White Paper, Annex 1 B.]

A still more important piece of evidence is the carefully prepared confidential communication, which the Imperial Chancellor sent to the Federated Governments of Germany shortly after the Servian reply was given.

In this confidential communication, which was nothing less than a call to arms to the entire German Empire, and which probably intended to convey the intimation that without formal mobilization the constituent states of Germany should begin to prepare for eventualities, von Bethmann-Hollweg recognized the possibility that Russia might feel it a duty "to take the part of Servia in her dispute with Austria-Hungary." Why, again, if Austria's case was so clearly justified?

The Imperial Chancellor added that

if Russia feels constrained to take sides with Servia in this conflict, she certainly has a right to do it,

but added that if Russia did this it would in effect challenge the integrity of the Austro-Hungarian Monarchy, and that Russia would therefore alone

bear the responsibility if a European war arises from the Austro-Servian question, which all the rest of the great European Powers wish to localize.

In this significant confidential communication the German Chancellor declares the strong interest which Germany had in the punishment of Servia by Austria. He says, "our closest interests therefore summon us to the side of Austria-Hungary," and he adds that

if contrary to hope, the trouble should spread, owing to the intervention of Russia, then, true to our duty as an Ally, we should have to support the neighboring monarchy with the entire might of the German Empire.[13]

[Footnote 13: German White Paper, Annex 2.]

It staggers ordinary credulity to believe that this portentous warning to the constituents of the German Empire to prepare for "the Day" should not have been written with advance knowledge of the Austrian ultimatum, which had only been issued on July 23d and only reached the other capitals of Europe on July 24th. The subsequent naive disclaimer by the German Foreign Office of any expectation that Austria's attack upon Servia could possibly have any interest to other European Powers is hardly consistent with its assertion that Germany's "closest interests" were involved in the question, or the portentous warnings to the States of the Empire to prepare for eventualities.

The German Ambassador to the United States who attempted early in the controversy and with disastrous results, to allay the rising storm of indignation in that country, formally admitted in an article in the Independent of September 7, 1914, that Germany "did approve in advance the Austrian ultimatum to Servia."

Why then was Germany guilty of duplicity in disclaiming, concurrently with its issuance, any such responsibility? The answer is obvious. This was necessary to support its contention that the quarrel between Austria and Servia was purely "local."

NOTE.--In Chapter VII it will appear from the French Yellow Bookthat the Prime Minister of Bavaria had knowledge of the Austrian ultimatum before its delivery in Belgrade.

CHAPTER V

THE ULTIMATUM TO SERVIA

To convince any reasonable man that this Austrian ultimatum to Servia was brutal in its tone and unreasonable in its demands, and that the reply of Servia was as complete an acquiescence as Servia could make without a fatal compromise of its sovereignty and self-respect, it is only necessary to print in parallel columns the demands of Austria and the reply of Servia.

AUSTRIA'S ULTIMATUM TO SERVIA

"To achieve this end the Imperial and Royal Government sees itself compelled to demand from the Royal Servian Government a formal assurance that it condemns this dangerous propaganda against the Monarchy; in other words, the whole series of tendencies, the ultimate aim of which is to detach from the Monarchy territories belonging to it, and that it undertakes to suppress by every means this criminal and terrorist propaganda.

"In order to give a formal character to this undertaking the Royal Servian Government shall publish on the front page of its 'Official Journal' of the 26th July, the following declaration:

"'The Royal Government of Servia condemns the propaganda directed against Austria-Hungary--i.e., the general tendency of which the final aim is to detach from the Austro-Hungarian Monarchy territories belonging to it, and it sincerely deplores the fatal consequence of these criminal proceedings.

"'The Royal Government regrets that Servian officers and functionaries participated in the above-mentioned propaganda, and thus compromised the good neighborly relations to which the Royal Government was solemnly pledged by its declaration of the 31st March, 1909.

"'The Royal Government, which disapproves and repudiates all idea of interfering or attempting to interfere with the destinies of the inhabitants of any part whatsoever of Austria-Hungary, considers it its duty formally to warn officers and functionaries, and the whole population of the kingdom, that henceforward it will proceed with the utmost rigor against persons who may be guilty of such machinations, which it will use all its efforts to anticipate and suppress.'

"This declaration shall simultaneously be communicated to the Royal Army as an order of the day by His Majesty the King and shall be published in the 'Official Bulletin' of the Army.

"'The Royal Servian Government further undertakes:

"1. To suppress any publication which incites to hatred and contempt of the Austro-Hungarian Monarchy and the general tendency of which is directed against its territorial integrity;

"2. To dissolve immediately the society styled Narodna Odbrana, to confiscate all its means of propaganda, and to proceed in the same manner against other societies and their branches in Servia which engage in propaganda against the Austro-Hungarian Monarchy. The Royal Government shall take the necessary measures to prevent the societies dissolved from continuing their activity under another name and form;

"3. To eliminate without delay from public instruction in Servia, both as regards the teaching body and also as regards the methods of instruction, everything that serves, or might serve, to foment the propaganda against Austria-Hungary:

"4. To remove from the military service, and from the administration in general, all officers and functionaries guilty of propaganda against the Austro-Hungarian Monarchy whose names and deeds the Austro-Hungarian Government reserves to itself the right of communicating to the Royal Government;

"5. To accept the collaboration in Servia of representatives of the Austro-Hungarian Government in the suppression of the subversive movement directed against the territorial integrity of the Monarchy;

"6. To take judicial proceedings against accessories to the plot of the 28th June who are on Servian territory. Delegates of the Austro-Hungarian Government will take part in the investigation relating thereto;

"7. To proceed without delay to the arrest of Major Voija Tankositch and of the individual named Milan Ciganovitch, a Servian State employ? who have been compromised by the results of the magisterial enquiry at Serajevo;

"8. To prevent by effective measures the cooperation of the Servian authorities in the illicit traffic in arms and explosives across the frontier, to dismiss and punish severely the officials of the frontier service at Schabatz and Loznica guilty of having assisted the perpetrators of the Serajevo crime by facilitating their passage across the frontier;

"9. To furnish the Imperial and Royal Government with explanations regarding the unjustifiable utterances of high Servian officials, both in Servia and abroad, who, notwithstanding their official position, did not hesitate after the crime of the 28th June to express themselves in interviews in terms of hostility to the Austro-Hungarian Government; and finally,

"10. To notify the Imperial and Royal Government without delay of the execution of the measures comprised under the preceding heads.

"The Austro-Hungarian Government expects the reply of the Royal Government at the latest by six o'clock on Saturday evening, the 25th July."

"The Royal Servian Government is of the opinion that it is mutually advantageous not to hinder the settlement of this question, and therefore, in case the Austro-Hungarian Government should not consider itself satisfied with this answer, it is ready as always to accept a peaceful solution, either by referring the decision of this question to the international tribunal at The Hague, or by leaving it to the great Powers who cooperated in the preparation of the explanation given by the Servian Government on the 17th-31st March, 1909."

THE SERVIAN REPLY

"The Royal Government has received the notification of the Austro-Hungarian Government of the 10th inst., and is convinced that its answer will remove every misunderstanding that threatens to disturb the pleasant neighborly relations between the Austro-Hungarian Monarchy and the Servian Kingdom.

"The Royal Government is certain that in dealing with the great neighboring monarchy these protests have under no pretexts been renewed which formerly were made both in the Skupshtina and in explanations and negotiations of responsible representatives of the State, and which, through the declaration of the Servian Government of March 18, 1909, were settled; furthermore, that since that time none of the various successive Governments of the kingdom, nor any of its officers, has made an attempt to change the political and legal conditions set up in Bosnia and Herzegovina. The Royal Government is certain that the Austro-Hungarian Government has made no representations of any kind along this line except in the case of a textbook concerning which the Austro-Hungarian Government received an entirely satisfactory reply. Servia, during the Balkan crisis, gave evidence in numerous cases of her pacific and temperate policies, and it will be thanks to Servia alone and the sacrifices that she alone made in the interest of European peace if that peace continue.

"The Royal Government cannot be held responsible for utterances of a private character such as newspaper articles and the peaceful work of societies, utterances which are quite ordinary in almost all countries, and which are not generally under State control, especially since the Royal Government, in the solution of a great number of questions that came up between Servia and Austria-Hungary, showed much consideration as a result of which most of these questions were settled in the best interests of the progress of the two neighboring countries.

"The Royal Government was therefore painfully surprised to hear the contention that Servian subjects had taken part in the preparations for the murder committed in Serajevo. It had hoped to be invited to cooperate in the investigations following this crime, and was prepared, in order to prove the entire correctness of its acts, to proceed against all persons concerning whom it had received information.

"In conformity with the wish of the Austro-Hungarian Government, the Royal Government is prepared to turn over to the court, regardless of station or rank, any Servian subject concerning whose participation in the crime at Serajevo proofs may be given to it. The Government pledges itself especially to publish on the first page of the official organ of July 26th the following declaration:

"'The Royal Servian Government condemns every propaganda that may be directed against Austria-Hungary; that is to say, all efforts designed ultimately to sever territory from the Austro-Hungarian Monarchy, and it regrets sincerely the sad consequences of these criminal machinations.'

"The Royal Government regrets that, in accordance with advices from the Austro-Hungarian Government, certain Servian officers and functionaries are taking an active part in the present propaganda, and that they have thereby jeopardized the pleasant neighborly relations to the maintenance of which the Royal Government was formally pledged by the declaration of March 31, 1909.

"The Government (what follows here is similar to the text demanded).

"The Royal Government further pledges itself:

"1. To introduce a provision in the press law on the occasion of the next regular session of the Skupshtina, according to which instigations to hatred and contempt of the Austro-Hungarian Monarchy, as well as any publication directed in general against the territorial integrity of Austria-Hungary, shall be punished severely.

"The Government pledges itself, on the occasion of the coming revision of the Constitution, to add to Article XXII. a clause permitting the confiscation of publications, the confiscation of which, under the present Article XXII. of the Constitution, would be impossible.

"2. The Government possesses no proof--and the Note of the Austro-Hungarian Government provides it with none--that the 'Narodna Odbrana' Society and other similar associations have up to the present committed any criminal acts through any of their members. Nevertheless, the Royal Government will accept the demand of the Austro-Hungarian Government and dissolve the Narodna Odbrana Society, as well as all societies that may work against Austria-Hungary.

"3. The Royal Servian Government agrees to eliminate forthwith from public education in Servia everything that might help the propaganda against Austria-Hungary, provided that the Austro-Hungarian Government gives it actual proof of this propaganda.

"4. The Royal Government is also ready to discharge from military and civil service such officers--provided it is proved against them by legal investigation--who have implicated themselves in acts directed against the territorial integrity of the Austro-Hungarian Monarchy; the Government expects that, for the purpose of instituting proceedings, the Austro-Hungarian Government will impart the names of these officers and employ 閣 and the acts of which they are accused.

"5. The Royal Servian Government must confess that it is not quite clear as to the sense and scope of the desire of the Austro-Hungarian Government to the effect that the Royal Servian Government bind itself to allow the cooperation within its territory of representatives of the Austro-Hungarian Government, but it nevertheless declares itself willing to permit such cooperation as might be in conformity with international law and criminal procedure, as well as with friendly neighborly relations.

"6. The Royal Government naturally holds itself bound to institute an investigation against all such persons as were concerned in the plot of June 15th-28th, or are supposed to have been concerned in it, and are on Servian soil. As to the cooperation of special delegates of the Austro-Hungarian

Government in this investigation, the Servian Government cannot accept such cooperation, since this would be a violation of the laws and criminal procedure. However, in individual cases, information as to the progress of the investigation might be given to the Austro-Hungarian delegates.

"7. On the very evening on which your Note arrived the Royal Government caused the arrest of Major Voislar Tankosic. But, regarding Milan Ciganovic, who is a subject of the Austro-Hungarian Monarchy, and who was employed until June 15th (as candidate) in the Department of Railroads it has not been possible to arrest this man up till now, for which reason a warrant has been issued against him.

"The Austro-Hungarian Government is requested, in order that the investigation may be made as soon as possible, to make known in the specified form what grounds of suspicion exist, and the proofs of guilt collected at the investigation in Serajevo.

"8. The Servian Government will increase the severity and scope of its measures against the smuggling of arms and explosives.

"It goes without saying that it will at once start an investigation and mete out severe punishment to the frontier officials of the Sabac-Loznica line who failed in their duty and allowed those responsible for the crime to cross the frontier.

"9. The Royal Government is willing to give explanations of the statements made in interviews by its officials in Servia and foreign countries after the crime, and which, according to the Austro-Hungarian Government, were anti-Austrian, as soon as the said Government indicates where these statements were made, and provides proofs that such statements were actually made by the said officials. The Royal Government will itself take steps to collect the necessary proofs and means of transmission for this purpose.

"10. The Royal Government will, in so far as this has not already occurred in this Note, inform the Austro-Hungarian Government of the taking of the measures concerning the foregoing matters, as soon as such measures have been ordered and carried out.

It increases the ineffaceable discredit of this brutal ultimatum when we consider the relative size of the two nations. Austria has a population of over 50,000,000 and Servia about 4,000,000. Moreover, Servia had just emerged from two terrible conflicts, from which it was still bleeding to exhaustion. Austria's ultimatum was that of a Goliath to David, and, up to the hour that this book goes to press, the result has not been different from that famous conflict.

Germany itself had already given to Servia an intimation of its intended fate. It had anticipated the Austrian ultimatum by some pointed suggestions to Servia on its own account, for in the letter already quoted from Sir M. de Bunsen to Sir Edward Grey, we learn that the German Secretary of State told the British Ambassador before the ultimatum was issued that he

on several occasions, in conversation with the Servian Minister, emphasized the extreme importance that Austro-Servian relations should be put on a proper footing.[14]

[Footnote 14: In English White Paper, No. 2.]

This pointed intimation from Germany, thus preceding the formal ultimatum from Austria, naturally gave Servia a quick appreciation that within the short space allowed by the ultimatum, it must either acquiesce in grossly unreasonable demands or perish as an independent nation.

To appreciate fully the brutality of this ultimatum let us imagine a precise analogy.

The relations of France and Germany--leaving aside the important difference of relative size--are not unlike the relations that existed between Servia and Austria. In 1908, Austria had forcibly annexed Bosnia and Herzegovina, both of them Slav countries, and when Servia had emerged from the Balko-Turkish War with signal credit to itself, it was again Austria that had intervened and deprived it of the fruit of its victories by denying it access to the sea.

Similarly, by the Treaty of Frankfort, Germany had forcibly annexed Alsace and Lorraine from France. As there existed in Servia voluntary organizations of men, which ceaselessly agitated for the recovery of Bosnia and

Herzegovina, so in France similar patriotic organizations have for the last forty years continuously agitated for a war which would lead to the ultimate recovery of Alsace and Lorraine. The statue of Strassburg in the Place de la Concorde has been covered with the emblems of mourning from the time that Bismarck wrung from Jules Favre the cession of the Rhine territory. If Austria's grievance against Servia were just, Germany has an equal and similar grievance against France.

Under these circumstances let us suppose that on the occasion of the visit of the German Crown Prince to Strassburg, that an Alsatian citizen of German nationality, having strong French sympathies, had assassinated the Crown Prince, and that France had formally disclaimed any complicity in the assassination and expressed its sympathy and regret.

Mutatis mutandis, let us suppose that Germany had thereupon issued to France the same ultimatum that Austria issued to Servia, requiring France to acknowledge moral responsibility for a crime, which it steadily disavowed. The ultimatum to France in that event would have included a peremptory demand that the government of France, a proud and self-respecting country, should publish in the Official Journal, and communicate as an "order of the day" to the army of France, a statement that the French Government formally denounced all attempts to recover Alsace and Lorraine; that it regretted the participation of French officers in the murder of the German Crown Prince; that it engaged to suppress in the Press of France any expressions of hatred or contempt for Germany; that it would dissolve all patriotic societies that have for their object the recovery of the "lost provinces"; that it would eliminate from the public schools of France all instruction which served to foment feeling against Germany; that it would remove from its army all officers who had joined in the agitation against Germany; that it would accept in the courts of France the participation of German officials in determining who were guilty, either of the Strassburg murder or of the propaganda for the recovery of Alsace and Lorraine; that it would further proceed to arrest and punish certain French officers, whom the German Government charged with participating in the offensive propaganda, and that it would furnish the German Government with full explanations and information in reference to its execution of these peremptory demands.

Let us suppose that such an ultimatum having been sent, that France had been given forty-eight hours to comply with conditions which were obviously fatal to its self-respect and forever destructive of its prestige as a great Power.

Can it be questioned what the reply of France or the judgment of the world would be in such a quarrel?

Every fair-minded man would say without hesitation that such an ultimatum would be an unprecedented outrage upon the fine proprieties of civilized life.

The only difference between the two cases is the fact that in the case of Germany and France the power issuing the ultimatum would be less than double the size of that nation which it sought to coerce, while in the case of Austria and Servia, the aggressor was twelve times as powerful as the power whose moral prestige and political independence it sought to destroy.

In view of the nature of these demands, the assurance which Austria subsequently gave Russia, that she would do nothing to lessen the territory of Servia, goes for nothing. From the standpoint of Servia, it would have been far better to lose a part of its territory and keep its independence and self-respect as to the remainder, than to retain all its existing land area, and by submitting to the ultimatum become virtually a vassal state of Austria. Certainly if Servia had acquiesced fully in Austria's demands without any qualification or reservation (as for the sake of peace it almost did), then Austria would have enjoyed a moral protectorate over all of Servia's territory, and its ultimate fate might have been that of Bosnia and Herzegovina, which Austria first governed as a protectorate, and later forcibly annexed.

CHAPTER VI

THE PEACE PARLEYS

The issuance of the Austrian ultimatum precipitated a grave crisis. It did not, however, present any insoluble problem. Peace could and should have been preserved. Its preservation is always possible when nations, which may be involved in a controversy, are inspired by a reasonably pacific purpose. Only when the masses of the people are inflamed with a passionate desire for war, and in a time of popular hysteria responsible statesmen are helplessly borne along the turgid flow of events as bubbles are carried by the swift current of a swollen river, is peace a visionary dream.

It is the peculiarity of the present crisis that no such popular hysteria existed. No popular demand for war developed until after it was virtually precipitated. Even then large classes of workingmen, both in Germany and France, protested.

The peoples of the various countries had scant knowledge of the issues which had been raised by their diplomats and had little, if any, interest in the Servian trouble. The chief exception to this was in Austria, where unquestionably popular feeling had been powerfully excited by the murder of the Archduke and where there had been, especially in Vienna, popular manifestations in favor of war. In Russia also there was not unnaturally a strong undercurrent of popular sympathy for Servia.

The writer was in the Engadine at the time referred to, and cosmopolitan St. Moritz, although a little place, was, in its heterogeneous population, Europe in microcosmic form. There the average man continued to enjoy his mid-summer holiday and refused to believe that so great a catastrophe was imminent until the last two fateful days in July. The citizens of all nations continued to fraternize, and were one in amazement that a war could be precipitated on causes in which the average man took so slight an interest.

Unembarrassed by any popular clamor, this war could have been prevented, and the important question presents itself to the Supreme Court of Civilization as to the moral responsibility for the failure of the negotiations.

Which of the two groups of powers sincerely worked for peace and which obstructed those efforts?

In reaching its conclusion our imaginary Court would pay little attention to mere professions of a desire for peace. A nation, like an individual, can covertly stab the peace of another while saying, "Art thou in health, my brother?" and even the peace of civilization can be betrayed by a Judas-kiss. Professions of peace belong to the cant of diplomacy and have always characterized the most bellicose of nations.

No war in modern times has been begun without the aggressor pretending that his nation wished nothing but peace, and invoking divine aid for its murderous policy. To paraphrase the words of Lady Teazle on a noted occasion, when Sir Joseph Surface talked much of "honor," it might be as well in such instances to leave the name of God out of the question.

The writer will so far anticipate the conclusions, which he thinks these records indisputably show, as to suggest the respective attitudes of the different groups of diplomats and statesmen as revealed by these papers. If the reader will realize fully the policy which from the first animated Germany and Austria, then the documents hereinafter quoted will acquire new significance.

Germany and Austria had determined to impose their will upon Servia, even though it involved a European war. From the outset they clearly recognized such a possibility and were willing to accept the responsibility.

The object to be gained was something more than a neutralization of the pro-Slav propaganda. It was to subject Servia to such severe punitive measures that thereafter her independence of will and moral sovereignty would be largely impaired, if not altogether destroyed. To do this it was not enough to have Servia take measures to prevent pro-Slav agitation within her borders. Austria neither wanted nor expected the acceptance of her impossible ultimatum.

It planned to submit such an ultimatum as Servia could not possibly accept and, to make this result doubly sure, it was thought desirable to give not only Servia but Europe the minimum time to take any preventive measures. Giving to Servia only forty-eight hours within which to reach a decision and to Europe barely twenty-four hours to protect the peace of the world, it was thought that Servia would do one of two things, either of which would be of incalculable importance to Germany and Austria.

If Servia accepted the ultimatum for lack of time to consider it, then its self-respect was hopelessly compromised and its independence largely destroyed. Thenceforth she would be, at least morally, a mere vassal of Austria.

If, however, Servia declined to accept the ultimatum, then war would immediately begin and Servia would be, as was thought, speedily subjected to punitive measures of such a drastic character that the same result would be attained.

From the commencement, both Germany and Austria recognized the possibility that Russia might intervene to protect Servia. To prevent this it was important that Russia and her allies of the Triple Entente should be given as little time as possible to consider their action, and it was thought that this would probably lead to Russia's acquiescence in the punishment of Servia and, if so, France and England, having no direct interest in Servia, would also undoubtedly acquiesce.

If, however, slow-moving Russia, instead of acquiescing, as she did in 1908 in the case of Bosnia and Herzegovina, should take up the gauntlet which Germany and Austria had thrown down, then it was all important to Germany and Austria that Russia should seem to be the aggressor.

For this there were two substantial reasons: the one was Italy and the other was England. Germany and Austria desired the cooperation of Italy and could not claim it as of right under the terms of the Triple Alliance, unless they were attacked. Upon the other hand, if England believed that Russia and France had declared war upon Germany and Austria, there was little probability of her intervention. For these reasons it was important that Germany and Austria should impress both England and Italy that their purposes were sincerely pacific and that on the other hand they should so clearly provoke Russia and France that those nations would declare war.

If the reader will keep this Janus-faced policy steadily in mind, he will understand the apparent inconsistencies in the diplomatic representations of the German Foreign Office. He will understand why Germany and Austria, while at times flouting Russia in the most flagrant manner and refusing her the common courtesies of diplomatic intercourse, were at the same time giving to England the most emphatic assurance of pacific intentions.

With this preliminary statement, let the record speak for itself. We have seen that the first great, and as events proved, fatal obstacle to peace which Germany interposed was practically contemporaneous with the issuance of the ultimatum. Germany did not wait for any efforts at conciliation. On the contrary, it attempted to bar effectually all such efforts by serving notice upon France, England, and Russia almost simultaneously with the issuance of the Austrian ultimatum,

that the acts as well as the demands of the Austro-Hungarian Government cannot but be looked upon as justified;

and the communication concluded:

We strongly desire that the dispute be localized, since any intervention of any Power on account of the various alliance obligations would bring consequences impossible to measure.[15]

[Footnote 15: German White Paper, Annex, 1 B.]

This had only one meaning. Austria was to be left to discipline Servia at will, or there would be war. Germany did not even wait for any suggestion of intervention, whether conciliatory or otherwise, but sought to interpose to any plan of peace, short of complete submission, an insuperable barrier by this threat of war. With this pointed threat to Europe, the next move was that of Russia, and it may be remarked that throughout the entire negotiations Russian diplomacy was more than equal to that of Germany.

Russia contented itself in the first instance by stating on the morning of July 24th, that Russia could not remain indifferent to the Austro-Servian conflict. This attitude could not surprise any one, for Russia's interest in the Balkans was well known and its legitimate concern in the future of any Slav state was, as Sir Edward Grey had said in Parliament in March, 1913, "a commonplace in European diplomacy in the past."

With this simple statement of its legitimate interest in a matter affecting the balance of power in Europe, Russia, instead of issuing an ultimatum or declaring war, as Germany and Austria may have hoped, joined with England in asking for a reasonable extension of time for all the Powers to concert for the preservation of peace. On July 24th, the very day that the Austrian ultimatum had reached St. Petersburg, the Russian Foreign Minister transmitted to the Austrian Government through its Charg?in Vienna the following communication:

The communication of the Austro-Hungarian Government to the Powers the day after the presentation of the ultimatum to Belgrade leaves to the Powers a delay entirely insufficient to undertake any useful steps whatever for the straightening out of the complications that have arisen. To prevent the incalculable consequences, equally disastrous for all the Powers, which can follow the method of action of the Austro-Hungarian Government, it seems indispensable to us that above all the delay given to Servia to reply should be extended. Austria-Hungary, declaring herself disposed to inform the Powers of the results of the inquiry upon which the Imperial and Royal Government bases its accusations, should at least give them also the time to take note of them (de s'en rendre compte). In this case, if the Powers should convince themselves of the well-groundedness of certain of the Austrian demands they would find themselves in a position to send to the Servian Government consequential advice. A refusal to extend the terms of the ultimatum would deprive of all value the step taken by the Austro-Hungarian Government in regard to the Powers and would be in contradiction with the very bases of international relations.[16]

[Footnote 16: Russian Orange Paper, No. 4.]

Could any court question the justice of this contention? The peace of the world was at stake. Time only was asked to see what could be done to preserve that peace and satisfy Austria's grievances to the uttermost.

Germany had only to intimate to Austria that "a decent respect to the opinions of mankind," as well as common courtesy to great and friendly nations, required that sufficient time be given not only to Servia, but to the other nations, to concert for the common good, especially as the period was one of mid-summer dullness, and many of the leading rulers and statesmen were absent from their respective capitals.

If Germany made any communication to Austria in the interests of peace the text has yet to be disclosed to the world. A word from Berlin to Vienna would have given the additional time which, with sincerely pacific intentions, might have resulted in the preservation of peace. Germany, so far as the record discloses, never spoke that word.

England had already anticipated the request of Russia that a reasonable time should be given to all interested parties. When the Austrian Minister in London handed the ultimatum to Sir Edward Grey on July the 24th, the following conversation took place, which speaks for itself:

In the ensuing conversation with his Excellency I (Sir Edward Grey) remarked that it seemed to me a matter for great regret that a time limit, and such a short one at that, had been insisted upon at this stage of the proceedings. The murder of the Archduke and some of the circumstances respecting Servia quoted in the note aroused sympathy with Austria, as was but natural, but at the same time I had never before seen one State address to another independent State a document of so formidable a character. Count Mensdorff replied that the present situation might never have arisen if Servia had held out a hand after the murder of the Archduke. Servia had, however, shown no sign of sympathy or help, though some weeks had already elapsed since the murder; a time limit, said his Excellency, was essential, owing to the procrastination on Servia's part.

I said that if Servia had procrastinated in replying a time limit could have been introduced later; but, as things now stood, the terms of the Servian reply had been dictated by Austria, who had not been content to limit herself to a demand for a reply within a limit of forty-eight hours from its presentation.

Unfortunately both Russia and England's requests for time were refused, on the plea that they had reached the Austrian Foreign Minister too late, although it has never yet been explained why, even if Count Berchtold were unable to take up the requests before the expiration of the ultimatum, the matter might not have been reopened for a few days by a corresponding extension of the time limit.

In the absence of some explanation, which as yet remains to be made, the absence of the Austrian Premier from Vienna at the time intervening between the issuance of the ultimatum and the expiration of the time limit seems like an extraordinarily petty piece of diplomatic finesse. He had without any warning to the great Powers of Europe, launched a thunderbolt, and if there ever was a time when a pacific foreign minister should have been at his post and open to suggestions of peace, it was in those two critical days. And yet, after issuing the ultimatum, he immediately takes himself beyond reach of personal parleys by going to Ischl, and this was taken by the German Foreign Office as a convenient excuse for an anticipated failure to extend this courtesy to Russia and England. Upon this we have the testimony of the English Ambassador at Berlin, who in his report to Sir Edward Grey, dated July 25th, says:

[The German] Secretary of State for Foreign Affairs says that on receipt of a telegram at ten o'clock this morning from German Ambassador at London, he immediately instructed German Ambassador at Vienna to pass on to the Austrian Minister for Foreign Affairs your suggestion, for an extension of time limit, and to speak to his Excellency about it. Unfortunately it appeared from the press that Count Berchtold is at Ischl, and Secretary of State thought that in these circumstances there would be delay and difficulty in getting time limit extended. Secretary of State said that he did not know what Austria-Hungary had ready on the spot, but he admitted quite freely that Austro-Hungarian Government wished to give the Servians a lesson, and that they meant to take military action. He also admitted that Servian Government could not swallow certain of the Austro-Hungarian demands....

A like excuse is found in a conversation with the Russian Charg?at Berlin, in which Bethmann-Hollweg expressed the fear "that in consequence of the absence of Berchtold at Ischl, and seeing the lack of time, his (Bethmann-Hollweg's telegrams suggesting delay) will remain without result."[17]

[Footnote 17: Russian Orange Paper, No. 14.]

These conversations are most illuminating. They refer to instructions to the German Ambassador in Vienna, which are not found in the German White Paper, although they would have thrown a searchlight upon the sincerity with which Germany "passed on" the most important request of England and Russia for a little time to save the peace of Europe, and it strongly suggests the possibility that Count Berchtold's most inopportune absence in Ischl was to be the excuse for the gross discourtesy of refusing to give any extension of time.

Kudachef, the Russian Charg?at Vienna, did not content himself with submitting the request to the Acting Foreign Minister (Baron Macchio) but to deprive Austria of the flimsy excuse of Berchtold's absence at Ischl, the

Russian Charg?went over the head of the Austrian Acting Foreign Minister and telegraphed the request for time to Count Berchtold at Ischl. Let the record tell for itself how this most reasonable request was made and refused.

The Russian Charg?sent on July 25th the two following telegrams to the Russian Foreign Minister:

Count Berchtold is at Ischl. Seeing the impossibility of arriving there in time, I have telegraphed him our proposal to extend the delay of the ultimatum, and I have repeated it verbally to Baron Macchio. This latter promised me to communicate it in time to the Minister of Foreign Affairs, but added that he could predict with assurance a categorical refusal.[18]

[Footnote 18: Russian Orange Paper, No. 11.]

Sequel to my telegram of to-day. Have just received from Macchio the negative reply of the Austro-Hungarian Government to our proposal to prolong the delay of the note.[19]

[Footnote 19: Russian Orange Paper, No. 12.]

It is evident from the Russian Orange Paper that that country had no illusions as to the possibility of a peaceful outcome. Germany has contended that on July the 24th, before Count Berchtold made his inopportune visit to Ischl, he sent for the Russian Charg?at Vienna and assured him that the punitive measures which Austria had determined to take against Servia at all costs would not involve any territorial acquisitions.

Of this interview the chief evidence comes indirectly from two sources, which are not entirely in accord.

In a telegram from the German Ambassador at Vienna to the German Chancellor, dated July 24th, it is said:

Count Berchtold to-day summoned the Russian Charg?d'Affaires in order to explain to him in detail and in friendly terms the position of Austria regarding Servia. After going over the historical developments of the last few years, he laid stress on the statement that the monarchy did not wish to appear against

Servia in the role of a conqueror. He said that Austria-Hungary would demand no territory, that the step was merely a definitive measure against Servian machinations; that Austria-Hungary felt herself obliged to exact guarantees for the future friendly behavior of Servia toward the monarchy; that he had no intention of bringing about a shifting of the balance of power in the Balkans. The Charg?d'Affaires, who as yet had no instructions from St. Petersburg, took the explanations of the Minister ad referendum adding that he would immediately transmit them to Sazonof.[20]

[Footnote 20: German White Paper, No. 3.]

In a report of the same interview from the English Ambassador at Vienna to Sir Edward Grey, it is said:

Russian Charg?d'Affaires was received this morning by Minister for Foreign Affairs, and said to him, as his own personal view, that Austrian note was drawn up in a form rendering it impossible of acceptance as it stood, and that it was both unusual and peremptory in its terms. Minister of Foreign Affairs replied that Austrian Minister was under instructions to leave Belgrade unless Austrian demands were accepted integrally by 4 P.M. to-morrow. His Excellency added that Dual Monarchy felt that its very existence was at stake; and that the step taken had caused great satisfaction throughout the country. He did not think that objections to what had been done could be raised by any power.[21]

[Footnote 21: English White Papers, No. 7.]

It will be noted that in the report of the English Ambassador there is no suggestion of any disclaimer of an intention to take Servian territory.

In the Russian Orange Paper, we find no report from its representative at Vienna of any such interview and Austria has never produced any document or memorandum either of such an interview or of such a concession to Russia. It is probable that such a concession was made, as Germany contends, and if so, Russian diplomacy was far too keen to be led upon a false trail by this empty promise and as the evidences multiplied that Austria would not consider either an extension of time or any modification of its terms and that Germany was acting in complete accord and cooperated with her Ally, the probability of war was unmistakable.

Sazonof at once sent for the English and French Ambassadors, and the substance of the conference is embodied in the telegram from the British Ambassador at St. Petersburg to Sir Edward Grey, dated July 24th, which throws a strong light upon the double effort of Russia and France to preserve the peace and also as an obvious necessity to prepare for the more probable issue of war:

Minister for Foreign Affairs said that Austria's conduct was both provocative and immoral; she would never have taken such action unless Germany had first been consulted; some of her demands were quite impossible of acceptance. He hoped that his Majesty's Government would not fail to proclaim their solidarity with Russia and France.

The French Ambassador gave me to understand that France would fulfill all the obligations entailed by her alliance with Russia, if necessity arose, besides supporting Russia strongly in any diplomatic negotiations.

I said that I would telegraph a full report to you of what their Excellencies had just said to me. I could not, of course, speak in the name of his Majesty's Government, but personally I saw no reason to expect any declaration of solidarity from his Majesty's Government that would entail an unconditional engagement on their part to support Russia and France by force of arms. Direct British interests in Servia were nil, and a war on behalf of that country would never be sanctioned by British public opinion. To this M. Sazonof replied that we must not forget that the general European question was involved, the Servian question being but a part of the former, and that Great Britain could not afford to efface herself from the problems now at issue.

In reply to these remarks I observed that I gathered from what he said that his Excellency was suggesting that Great Britain should join in making a communication to Austria to the effect that active intervention by her in the internal affairs of Servia could not be tolerated. But, supposing Austria nevertheless proceeded to embark on military measures against Servia in spite of our representations, was it the intention of the Russian Government forthwith to declare war on Austria?

M. Sazonof said that he himself thought that Russian mobilization would at any rate have to be carried out; but a council of ministers was being held this afternoon to consider the whole question. A further council would be held, probably to-morrow, at which the Emperor would preside, when a decision would be come to....

Had England then followed the sagacious suggestion of Sazonof, would war have been averted?

Possibly, perhaps probably. Germany's principal fear was the intervention of England. In view of its supremacy on the seas this was natural. It was England's intimation in the Moroccan crisis of 1911, made in Lloyd George's Mansion House speech, which at that time induced Germany to reverse the engines. Might not the same intimation in 1914 have had a like effect upon the mad counsels of Potsdam? The answer can only be a matter of conjecture. It depends largely upon how deep-seated the purpose of Germany may have been to provoke a European war at a time when Russia, France, or England were not fully prepared.

It does not follow that if Sazonof was right, Sir Edward Grey was necessarily wrong in declining to align England definitely with Russia and France at that stage. He was the servant of a democratic nation and could not ignore the public opinion of his country as freely as the Russian Foreign Minister. To take such a course, it would have been necessary for Grey to submit the matter to Parliament, and while with a large liberal majority his policy might have been endorsed, yet it would have been after such an acrimonious discussion and such vehement protests that England would have stood before the world "as a house divided against itself."

Both Sazonof and Sir Edward Grey from their respective standpoints were right. Neither made a single false step in the great controversy.

As a result of this interview, Russia, England, and France, after the request for time had been abruptly refused, next proceeded in the interests of peace to persuade Servia to make as conciliatory a reply to the impossible ultimatum as was possible without a fatal compromise of her political independence.

While the lack of time prevented France and Russia from making any formal communication to Servia on the question, yet Sazonof had a conference with the Servian Minister and discussed the wisdom of avoiding an attack on Belgrade by having the Servian forces withdrawn to the interior and then appealing to the Powers, and Russia thereupon made the broad and magnanimous suggestion that if Servia should appeal to the Powers, Russia would be quite ready to stand aside and leave the question in the hands of England, France, Germany, and Italy.

This interview, as reported by the British Ambassador at St. Petersburg to Sir Edward Grey, dated July 25th, is as follows:

I saw the Minister for Foreign Affairs this morning, and communicated to his Excellency the substance of your telegram of to-day to Paris, and this afternoon, I discussed with him the communication which the French Ambassador suggested should be made to the Servian Government, as recorded in your telegram of yesterday to Belgrade....

The Minister for Foreign Affairs said that Servia was quite ready to do as you had suggested and to punish those proved to be guilty, but that no independent State could be expected to accept the political demands which had been put forward. The Minister for Foreign Affairs thought, from a conversation which he had with the Servian Minister yesterday, that in the event of the Austrians attacking Servia, the Servian Government would abandon Belgrade and withdraw their forces into the interior, while they would at the same time appeal to the Powers to help them. His Excellency was in favor of their making this appeal. He would like to see the question placed on an international footing, as the obligations taken by Servia in 1908, to which reference is made in the Austrian ultimatum, were given not to Austria, but to the Powers.

If Servia should appeal to the Powers, Russia would be quite ready to stand aside and leave the question in the hands of England, France, Germany, and Italy. It was possible, in his opinion, that Servia might propose to submit the question to arbitration.

Pursuant to this policy of conciliation Sir Edward Grey in direct communication with the Servian Minister at London, Mr. Crackenthorpe, the

British Ambassador at Belgrade, in direct communication with the Servian Foreign Ministry, and Sazonof in interviews with the Servian Minister at St. Petersburg, all brought direct influence upon Servia to make a conciliatory reply.

Thus Sir Edward Grey instructed Crackenthorpe:

Servia ought to promise that if it is proved that Servian officials, however subordinate they may be, were accomplices in the murder of the Archduke at Serajevo, she will give Austria the fullest satisfaction. She certainly ought to express concern and regret. For the rest, Servian Government must reply to Austrian demands as they consider best in Servian interests.

It is impossible to say whether military action by Austria when time limit expires can be averted by anything but unconditional acceptance of her demands, but only chance appears to lie in avoiding an absolute refusal and replying favorably to as many points as the time limit allows....

I have urged upon the German Ambassador that Austria should not precipitate military action.[22]

[Footnote 22: English White Paper, No. 12.]

In response to these suggestions, Mr. Crackenthorpe communicated Sir Edward Grey's pacific suggestions to the Servian Minister and received the following reply, as reported in Crackenthorpe's report to Sir Edward Grey, dated July 25th.

The Council of Ministers is now drawing up their reply to the Austrian note. I am informed by the Under Secretary of State for Foreign Affairs that it will be most conciliatory and will meet the Austrian demands in as large a measure as is possible....

The Servian Government consider that, unless the Austrian Government want war at any cost, they cannot but be content with the full satisfaction offered in the Servian reply.[23]

[Footnote 23: English White Paper, No. 21.]

These pacific suggestions to Servia met with complete success, and as a result that country on July 25th, and before the expiration of the ultimatum, made a reply to Austria which astonished the world with its spirit of conciliation and for a short time gave rise to optimistic hopes of peace.

At some sacrifice of its self-respect as a sovereign State, it accepted substantially the demands of Austria, with a few minor reservations, which it expressed its willingness to refer either to arbitration at The Hague Tribunal or to a conference of the Powers.[24]

[Footnote 24: English White Paper, No. 39.]

Neither Germany nor Austria seriously contended that the reply was not on its face a substantial acquiescence in the extreme Austrian demands. They contented themselves with impeaching the sincerity of the assurances, calling the concessions "shams." Unless Austria, in asking assurances from Servia, were content to accept them as made in good faith and allow their sincerity to be determined by future deeds, why should the ultimatum, calling for such assurances, have been made? If Germany and Austria had accepted Servia's reply as sufficient, and Servia had subsequently failed to fulfill its promises in the utmost good faith, there would have been little sympathy for Servia, and no general war. Russia and England pledged their influence to compel Servia, if necessary, to meet fully any reasonable demand of Austria. The principal outstanding question, which Servia agreed to arbitrate or leave to the Powers, was the participation of Austrian officials in the Servian courts. This did not present a difficult problem. Austria's professed desire for an impartial investigation could have been easily attained by having the Powers appoint a commission of neutral jurists to make such investigation.

In any event, Austria could have accepted the very substantial concessions of Servia and without prejudice to its rights proceeded to The Hague Tribunal or to a concert of the Powers as to the few and comparatively simple open points. When one recalls the infinite treasure of property and life, which would thus have been saved the world, had Germany and Austria accepted this reasonable and pacific course, one can only exclaim, "But oh, the pity of it!"

It is significant that while the entire official German press gave ample space to the Austrian ultimatum and rejoiced in Austria's energetic attitude, it withheld from the German people any adequate information as to the conciliatory nature of the Servian reply, for the Russian Charg?at Berlin telegraphed to Sazonof:

The Wolff Bureau has not published the text of the Servian response which was communicated to it. Up to this moment this note has not appeared in extenso in any of local journals, which according to all the evidence do not wish to give it a place in their columns, understanding the calming effect which this publication would produce upon the German readers.[25]

[Footnote 25: Russian Orange Paper, No. 46.]

Instead of getting the truth, the Berlin populace proceeded to make riotous demonstrations against the Russian and Servian Embassies.

The time limit on the ultimatum expired on July the 25th at six o'clock in the evening.

There is no more significant and at the same time discreditable feature of an infinitely discreditable chapter in history than that the Austrian Government, without giving the Servian answer the consideration even of a single hour, immediately severed all diplomatic intercourse with Belgrade and at 6.30 P.M. the Minister of Austria

informed the Servian Government by note that, not having received within the delay fixed a satisfactory response, he is leaving Belgrade with the whole personnel of the legation.

On the same night Austria ordered the mobilization of a considerable part of its army.

Notwithstanding these rebuffs, England, France, and Russia continued to labor for peace, and made further pacific suggestions, all of which fell upon deaf ears.

On July 25th, Sir Edward Grey proposed that the four Powers (England,

France, Italy, and Germany) should unite

in asking the Austrian and Russian Governments not to cross the frontier and to give time for the four Powers, acting at Vienna and St. Petersburg, to try and arrange matters. If Germany will adopt this view I feel strongly that France and ourselves should act upon it. Italy would no doubt gladly cooperate.[26]

[Footnote 26: English White Paper, Nos. 24 and 25.]

To this reasonable request the German Chancellor replied:

The distinction made by Sir Edward Grey between the Austro-Servian and Austro-Russian conflict is quite correct. We wish as little as England to mix in the first, and, first and last, we take the ground that this question must be localized by the abstention of all the Powers from intervention in it. It is therefore our earnest hope that Russia will refrain from any active intervention, conscious of her responsibility and of the seriousness of the situation. If an Austro-Russian dispute should arise, we are ready, with the reservation of our known duties as Allies, to cooperate with the other great Powers in mediation between Russia and Austria.[27]

[Footnote 27: German White Paper, Exhibit 13.]

This distinction is hard to grasp. It attempts to measure the difference between tweedledum and tweedledee. Russia's current difference with Austria concerned the attempt of the latter to crush Servia without interference. Russia claimed such right of intervention. Germany would not interfere in the former matter, but would abstractly but not concretely mediate between Russia and Austria in the latter. Mediate about what? To refuse to mediate over the Servian question was to refuse to mediate at all. For all practical purposes the two things were indistinguishable.

All that Germany did on July 25th, so far as the record discloses, was to "pass on" England's and Russia's requests for more time, but subsequent events indicate that it was "passed on" without any endorsement, for is it credible that Austria would have ignored its ally's request for more time if it had ever been made? Here again we note with disappointment the absence from the record of Germany's message to Austria, "passing on" the reasonable request for an extension of time. The result indicates that the request received, if any endorsement, the "faint praise" which is said to "damn."

Was ever the peace of the world shattered upon so slight a pretext? A little time, a few days, even a few hours, might have sufficed to preserve the world from present horrors, but no time could be granted. A snap judgment was to be taken by these pettifogging diplomats. The peace of the world was to be torpedoed by submarine diplomacy. The Austrian Government could wait nearly three months to try the assassin, who admittedly slew the Austrian Archduke, but could not wait even a few hours before condemning Servia to political death. It could not grant Russia any time to consider a matter gravely affecting its interests, even if the peace of Europe and the happiness of the world depended on it. It would be difficult to find in recorded history a greater discourtesy to a friendly Power, for Austria was not at war with Russia.

Defeated in their effort to get an extension of time, England, France, and Russia made further attempts to preserve peace by temporarily arresting military proceedings until further efforts toward conciliation could be made. Sir Edward Grey proposed to Germany, France, Russia, and Italy that they should unite in asking Austria and Servia not to cross the frontier "until we had had time to try and arrange matters between them," but the German Ambassador read Sir Edward Grey a telegram that he had received from the German Foreign Office saying

that his Government had not known beforehand, and had had no more than other Powers to do with the stiff terms of the Austrian note to Servia, but that once she had launched that note, Austria could not draw back. Prince Lichnowsky said, however, that if what I contemplated was mediation between Austria and Russia, Austria might be able with dignity to accept it. He expressed himself as personally favorable to this suggestion.

It will be noted that Germany thus gave to England, as it had already given to Russia and France in the most unequivocal terms, a disclaimer of any responsibility for the Austrian ultimatum, but we have already seen that when the German Foreign Office prepared its statement for the German nation, which was circulated in the Reichstag on August 4th, Germany confessed the insincerity of these assurances by admitting that before the ultimatum was issued the Austrian Government had advised the German Foreign Office of its intentions and asked its opinion and that

we were able to assure our ally most heartily of our agreement with her view of the situation and to assure her that any action that she might consider it necessary to take ... would receive our approval.

Here again it is to be noted that the telegram, which the German Foreign Office sent to Prince Lichnowsky, and which that diplomat simply read to Sir Edward Grey, is not set forth in the exhibits to the German White Paper.

As we have seen, Germany never, so far as the record discloses, sought in any way to influence Austria to make this or any concession until after the Kaiser's return from Norway and then only if we accept the assurances of its Foreign Office which are not supported by official documents. Its attitude was shown by the declaration of its Ambassador at Paris to the French Minister of Foreign Affairs, which, while again disclaiming that Germany had countenanced the Austrian ultimatum, yet added that Germany "approved" its point of view,

and that certainly, the arrow once sent, Germany could not allow herself to be guided except by her duty as ally.[28]

[Footnote 28: Russian Orange Paper, No. 19.]

This seemed to be the fatal error of Germany, that its duties to civilization were so slight that it should support its ally, Austria, whether the latter were right or wrong. Such was its policy, and it carried it out with fatal consistency. To support its ally in actual war without respect to the justice of the quarrel may be defensible, but to support it in a time of peace in an iniquitous demand and a policy of gross discourtesy to friendly States offends every sense of international morality.

On the following day Russia proposed to Austria that they should enter into an exchange of private views, with the object of an alteration in common of some clauses of the Austrian ultimatum. To this Austria never even replied.

The Russian Minister communicated this suggestion to the German Minister for Foreign Affairs and expressed the hope that he would "find it possible to advise Vienna to meet our proposal," but this did not accord with German policy, for on that day the German Ambassador in Paris called upon the French Minister of Foreign Affairs, and submitted the following formal declaration:

"Austria has declared to Russia that she does not seek territorial acquisitions, and that she does not threaten the integrity of Servia. Her only object is to insure her own tranquillity. Consequently it rests with Russia to avoid war. Germany feels herself at one with France in her keen desire to preserve the peace, and strongly hopes that France will use her influence at St. Petersburg in the direction of moderation." The [French] Minister observed that Germany could on her side take similar steps at Vienna, especially in view of the conciliatory spirit which Servia had shown. The Ambassador answered that that was not possible, in view of the resolution taken not to interfere in the Austro-Servian conflict. Thereupon the Minister asked if the four Powers-- England, Germany, Italy, and France--were not able to take steps at St. Petersburg and Vienna, since the affair reduced itself in essentials to a conflict between Russia and Austria. The Ambassador pleaded the absence of instructions. Finally, the Minister refused to adhere to the German proposal.[29]

[Footnote 29: Russian Orange Paper, No. 28.]

This significant interview states the consistent attitude of Germany. The burden is put upon France to induce its ally to desist from any intervention and thus give Austria a free hand, while Germany emphatically declines to promote the same pacific object by suggesting to Austria a more conciliatory course.

On the same day England asked France, Italy, and Germany to meet in London for an immediate conference to preserve the peace of Europe, and to this fruitful suggestion, which might have saved that peace, the German Secretary of State, after conferring with the British Ambassador at Berlin, replied that the conference

would practically amount to a court of arbitration and could not, in his opinion, be called together except at the request of Austria and Russia. He could not, therefore, fall in with your [Sir Edward Grey's] suggestion, desirous though he was to cooperate for the maintenance of peace. I [Sir E. Goschen] said I was sure that your idea had nothing to do with arbitration, but meant that representatives of the four nations not directly interested should discuss and suggest means for avoiding a dangerous situation. He [von Jagow] maintained, however, that such a conference as you proposed was not practicable.[30]

[Footnote 30: English White Paper, No. 43.]

Germany's refusal to have Servia's case submitted to the Powers even for their consideration is the more striking when it is recalled that on the same day the German Ambassador at London quoted the German Secretary of State as saying

that there were some things in the Austrian note that Servia could hardly be expected to accept,

thus recognizing that Austria's ultimatum was, at least in part, unjust. Sir Edward Grey then called the German Ambassador's attention to the fact that if Austria refused the conciliatory reply of Servia and marched into that country

it meant that she was determined to crush Servia at all costs, being reckless of the consequences that might be involved.

He added that the Servian reply

should at least be treated as a basis for discussion and pause,

and asked that the German Government should urge this at Vienna but, as we have already seen, the German Secretary of State had already replied that such a conference "was not practicable," and that it "would practically amount to a court of arbitration," and could not, in his opinion, be called together "except at the request of Austria and Russia."[31]

[Footnote 31: English White Paper, No. 16.]

That this was a mere evasion is perfectly plain. Germany already knew that Austria would not ask for such a conference, for Austria had already refused Russia's request for an extension of time and had actually commenced its military operations.

Germany's attitude is again clearly indicated by the letter of the Russian Minister in Germany to the Russian Foreign Office in which he states that on July 27th he called at the German Foreign Office and asked it,

to urge upon Vienna in a more pressing fashion to take up this line of conciliation. Von Jagow replied that he could not advise Austria to yield.[32]

[Footnote 32: Russian Orange Paper, No. 38.]

Why not? Russia and its allies had advised Servia to yield and Servia had conceded nearly every claim. Why could not the German Foreign Office advise Vienna to meet conciliation by conciliation, if its desire for peace were sincere?

Before this interview took place, the French Ambassador had called at the German Foreign Office on a similar errand and urged the English suggestion that action should at once be taken by England, Germany, Russia, and France at St. Petersburg and Vienna, to the effect that Austria and Servia

should abstain from any act which might aggravate the situation at the present hour.

By this was meant that there should be, pending further parleys, no invasion of Servia by Austria and none of Austria by Russia. To this the German Foreign Minister opposed a categorical refusal.

On the same day the Russian Ambassador at Vienna had "a long and earnest conversation" with the Austrian Under-Secretary of State for Foreign Affairs. He expressed the earnest hope that

something would be done before Servia was actually invaded. Baron Macchio replied that this would now be difficult, as a skirmish had already taken place on the Danube, in which the Servians had been aggressors.

The Russian Ambassador then said that his country would do all it could to keep the Servians quiet, "and even to fall back before an Austrian advance in order to gain time."

He urged that the Austrian Ambassador at St. Petersburg should be furnished with full powers to continue discussions with the Russian Minister for Foreign Affairs,

who was very willing to advise Servia to yield all that could be fairly asked of her as an independent Power.

The only reply to this reasonable suggestion was that it would be submitted to the Minister for Foreign Affairs.[33]

[Footnote 33: English White Paper, No. 56.]

On the same day the German Ambassador at Paris called upon the French Foreign Office and "strongly insisted on the exclusion of all possibility of mediation or a conference"[34]; and yet contemporaneously the Imperial German Chancellor was advising London that he had

started the efforts towards mediation in Vienna, immediately in the way desired by Sir Edward Grey, and had further communicated to the Austrian Foreign Minister the wish of the Russian Foreign Minister for a direct talk in Vienna.

[Footnote 34: Russian Orange Paper, No. 34.]

What hypocrisy! In the formal German defense, the German Foreign Office, after stating its conviction

that an act of mediation could not take into consideration the Austro-Servian conflict, which was purely an Austro-Hungarian affair,

claimed that Germany had transmitted Sir Edward Grey's further suggestion to Vienna, in which Austro-Hungary was urged either to agree to accept the Servian answer as sufficient or to look upon it as a basis for further conversations;

but the Austro-Hungarian Government--playing the role of the wicked partner of the combination--"in full appreciation of our mediatory activity" (so says the German White Paper with sardonic humor), replied to this proposition that, coming after the opening of hostilities, "it was too late."

Can it be fairly questioned that if Germany had done something more than merely "transmit" these wise and pacific suggestions, Austria would have complied with the suggestions of its powerful ally or that Austria would have suspended its military operations if Germany had given any intimation of such a wish?

On the following day, July 28th, the door was further closed on any possibility of compromise, when the Austrian Minister for Foreign Affairs

said, quietly, but firmly, that no discussion could be accepted on the basis of the Servian note; that war would be declared to-day, and that the well-known pacific character of the Emperor, as well as, he might add, his own, might be accepted as a guarantee that the war was both just and inevitable; that this was a matter that must be settled directly between the two parties immediately concerned.

To this arrogant and unreasonable contention that Europe must accept the guarantee of the Austrian Foreign Minister as to the righteousness of Austria's quarrel, the British Ambassador suggested "the larger aspect of the question," namely, the peace of Europe, and to this "larger aspect," which should have given any reasonable official some ground for pause, the Austrian Foreign Minister replied that he

had it also in mind, but thought that Russia ought not to oppose operations like those impending, which did not aim at territorial aggrandizement, and which could no longer be postponed.[35]

[Footnote 35: English White Paper, No. 62.]

The private conversations between Russia and Austria having thus failed, Russia returned to the proposition of a European conference to preserve its peace. Its Ambassador in Vienna on July 28th had a further conference with Berchtold and again earnestly pleaded for peace on the basis of friendly relations not only between Austria and Servia but between Austria and Russia. The conversation in the light of present developments is so significant that it bears quotation in extenso:

I pointed out to him in the most friendly terms how much it was desirable to find a solution which, while consolidating the good relations between Austria-Hungary and Russia, should give to the Austro-Hungarian Monarchy serious guarantees for its future relations with Servia.

I called the attention of Count Berchtold to all the dangers to the peace of Europe which would be brought about by an armed conflict between Austria-Hungary and Servia.

Count Berchtold replied that he understood perfectly well the seriousness of the situation and the advantages of a frank explanation with the Cabinet of St. Petersburg. He told me that on the other hand the Austro-Hungarian Government, which had only reluctantly decided upon the energetic measures which it had taken against Servia, could now neither withdraw nor enter upon any discussion of the terms of the Austro-Hungarian note.

Count Berchtold added that the crisis had become so acute and that public opinion had been excited to such a degree that the Government, even if it desired, could no longer consent to it, all the less, he said to me, because the very reply of Servia gave proof of the lack of sincerity in its promises for the future.

On the same day, July 28th, the German Imperial Chancellor sent for the English Ambassador and excused his failure to accept the proposed conference of the neutral Powers, on the ground that he did not think it would be effective,

because such a conference would, in his opinion, have the appearance of an "Areopagus" consisting of two Powers of each group sitting in judgment upon the two remaining Powers.

After engaging in this narrow and insincere quibble, and, being reminded of Servia's conciliatory reply,

his Excellency said that he did not wish to discuss the Servian note, but that Austria's standpoint, and in this he agreed, was that her quarrel with Servia was a purely Austrian concern, with which Russia had nothing to do.[36]

[Footnote 36: English White Paper, No. 71.]

At this stage of the controversy it will be noted that every proposal to preserve peace had come from the Triple Entente and that every such proposal had met with an uncompromising negative from Austria, and either that or obstructive quibbles from Germany.

CHAPTER VII

THE ATTITUDE OF FRANCE

Before proceeding to record the second and final stage in the peace parleys, in which the German Kaiser became the protagonist, it is desirable to interpolate the additional data, which the French Yellow Book has given to the world since the preceding chapter was written and the first editions of this book were printed. This can be done with little sacrifice to the chronological sequence of this narrative.

The evidence of the Yellow Book is fuller in scope and greater in detail than the other governmental publications, and while largely cumulative in its character, it serves to bring into a sharper light certain phases of this extraordinary controversy.

It has been prepared with great care by M. Jules Cambon, who was the French Ambassador at Berlin during the controversy, and MM. de Margerie and Berthelot, experienced and influential diplomats in the French Ministry of Foreign Affairs. It consists of 160 documents, classified into seven chapters, each dealing with different periods of time in the great controversy. The delay in its presentation is somewhat compensated by the exceptional fullness of the data which is thus submitted to the scrutiny of a candid world.

The French Yellow Book confirms the impression that France was most fortunate in having entrusted its interests at the difficult post of Berlin in this great crisis to so distinguished and experienced a diplomat as M. Jules Cambon.

Throughout the whole controversy the impartial reader is deeply impressed with the fact, which the more candid apologists for Germany are themselves disposed to admit, that Germany's chief weakness lay in its incapable diplomatic representatives. An interesting subject for conjecture suggests itself as to what would have happened if Prince Bismarck had been at the helm at this critical juncture. His guiding principles of statecraft with reference to foreign relations were to isolate the enemy, make him the apparent aggressor, and then crush him as effectually and speedily as possible. He never would have initiated this war. His nature was that of the fox as well as the lion.

In the years that have succeeded his dismissal, a certain dry rot, due to the tendency of the Prussian Government to distribute its diplomatic offices among highborn but incompetent Junkers,--une petite gentilhommerie pauvre et stupide, as Bismarck once described them--had affected the efficiency of German diplomacy. Feebly attempting to walk in the steps of the Iron Chancellor, they wittingly or unwittingly reversed Bismarck's policy by almost isolating Germany, consolidating its enemies, and then proceeding to attack them simultaneously. This may have been magnificent courage, but it was not wise statecraft. The might of the German sabre was supposed to offset these blundering disciples of Machiavelli.

Russia, England, and France were more fortunate and of their representatives few, if any, shone with greater intellectual distinction or moral courage than M. Jules Cambon. This distinguished diplomat had had exceptional experience in representing his country in various capitals of the world, and the author, who enjoyed the honor of his acquaintance, when he was accredited to Washington, already knew, what the documents in the French Yellow Book so clearly reveal, that Cambon was a diplomat of great intellectual ability. With acute sagacity he grasped the significance of the fateful events, in which he was a participant. To his calm and well-poised intellectuality he added a moral force, resulting from the clear integrity of his purpose and the broad humanity of his aims.

On more than one occasion he spoke "in the name of humanity," and in his constant attempt to convince the German Foreign Office as to its clear duty to civilization to preserve the peace of the world, he became the representative, not merely of France, but of civilization itself.

In this great diplomatic controversy, one of the greatest in the history of the world, the three representatives, who stand out with the greatest intellectual and moral distinction, are Sazonof, Grey, and Cambon.

The first displayed the greatest sagacity in divining from the very outset the real purposes of Germany and Austria and in checkmating the diplomatic moves, which sought to make Russia apparently the aggressor.

Sir Edward Grey's chief merit lay in his unwearying but ineffectual efforts to bring about a peaceful solution of the problem and also in the absolute candor--so unusual in diplomacy--with which he dealt on the one hand with the efforts of Russia and France to align England on their side at the beginning of the quarrel, and on the other, to continue friendly negotiations with Germany and Austria, without in any respect unfairly misleading them as to England's possible ultimate action.

The French Ambassador will justly receive the approval of posterity for the high courage and moral earnestness with which he pressed upon the German Foreign Office the inevitable consequences of its acts.

The first chapter of the French Yellow Book consists largely of communications written from Berlin by M. Jules Cambon in the year 1913. Its most interesting document is his report from Berlin under date November 22, 1913, as to a conversation between the Kaiser and the King of Belgium, with reference to a change in the pacific attitude, which Cambon had previously imputed to the Kaiser.

To the world at large this statement would be more convincing if the source of the information had been disclosed. Those who know M. Jules Cambon, however, will have a reasonable confidence that when he states that he received the record of this conversation "from an absolutely sure source," more than usual credence can be given to the statement. Reading between the lines, the implication is not unreasonable that the source of Cambon's authority was King Albert himself, but this rests only on a plausible conjecture.

The fact that so trained an observer as the French Ambassador had seen in the Kaiser a marked change as early as 1913 is significant, and history may justify Cambon in his shrewd conjecture that "the impatience of the soldiers," meaning thereby the German General Staff, and the growing popularity of his chauvinistic son, the Crown Prince, had appreciably modified the pacific attitude of the Kaiser, which had served the cause of peace so well in the Moroccan crisis. Cambon's recital of the incident in question, written on November 22, 1913, justifies quotation in extenso.

I have received from an absolutely sure source a record of a conversation which is reported between the Emperor and the King of the Belgians, in the presence of the Chief of the General Staff, General von Moltke, a fortnight ago--a conversation which would appear greatly to have struck King Albert. I am in no way surprised by the impression created, which corresponds with that made on me some time ago. Hostility against us is becoming more marked, and the Emperor has ceased to be a partisan of peace. The German Emperor's interlocutor thought up to the present, as did everybody, that William II., whose personal influence has been exerted in many critical circumstances in favor of the maintenance of peace, was still in the same state of mind. This time, it appears, he found him completely changed. The German Emperor is no longer in his eyes the champion of peace against the bellicose tendencies of certain German parties. William II. has been brought to think that war with France is inevitable, and that it will have to come one day or the other. The Emperor, it need hardly be said, believes in the crushing superiority of the German army and in its assured success.

General von Moltke spoke in exactly the same sense as his sovereign. He also declared that war was necessary and inevitable, but he showed himself still more certain of success. "For," said he to the King, "this time we must put an end to it" (cette fois il faut en finir), "and your Majesty can hardly doubt the irresistible enthusiasm which on that day will carry away the whole German people."

The King of the Belgians protested that to interpret the intentions of the

French Government in this manner was to travesty them, and to allow oneself to be misled as to the feelings of the French nation by the manifestations of a few hotheads, or of conscienceless intriguers.

The Emperor and his Chief of General Staff none the less persisted in their point of view.

During this conversation the Emperor, moreover, appeared overwrought, and irritable. As the years begin to weigh upon William II. the family traditions, the retrograde feelings of the Court, and, above all, the impatience of the soldiers, are gaining more ascendency over his mind. Perhaps he may feel I know not what kind of jealousy of the popularity acquired by his son, who flatters the passions of the Pan-Germans, and perhaps he may find that the position of the Empire in the world is not commensurate with its power. Perhaps, also, the reply of France to the last increase in the German army, the object of which was to place Germanic superiority beyond question, may count for something in these bitternesses, for whatever one may say it is felt here that the Germans cannot do much more. One may ask what lay behind the conversation. The Emperor and his Chief of General Staff may have intended to impress the King of the Belgians, and to lead him not to resist in case a conflict with us should arise[37]....

[Footnote 37: French Yellow Book, No. 6.]

This picture of the Kaiser is interesting and significant.

Germany's loss of prestige in the Moroccan controversy, due to the Kaiser's unwillingness to precipitate a war at that time and his somewhat diminished popularity with his people, not only accentuated the desire of his military camarilla to find another pretext for a war, but may have modified the Kaiser's resistance to this bellicose policy. Until that time he had been quite content to play the part of Caesar. It may be questioned whether he had previously a real desire to be a Caesar. To describe himself metaphorically as "clad in shining armor" and to shake the "mailed fist" was his constant pose. "And so he played his part." As long as the world was content to take this imperial fustian in a Pickwickian sense, the imperial impresario found the same enjoyment as when he staged Sardanapalus on the boards of the Berlin Theater.

The Kaiser was destined to stage a greater spectacle than the burning of a Babylonian palace. His crowning achievement was to apply the torch to civilization itself.

Prior to 1913 neither his wishes nor plans carried him further than the congenial art of imperial posing. Behind his natural preference for peace was ever the lurking fear that a disastrous war might cost him his throne. The experience of Napoleon the Third was quite too recent to be ignored.

In the Moroccan controversy, the unwillingness of France to assent to all demands and the resolute purpose of England to support its ally, presented a crisis, which could not be met with rhetorical phrases, and the Kaiser found himself confronted with a situation, in which a very considerable number of thoughtful and influential Germans favored an immediate appeal to arms, and as to which only his word was wanted to precipitate hostilities in 1911.

The Kaiser at that time failed to meet the expectations of those who had expected a more warlike attitude from the knight "clad in shining armor," and the expression "William the Peaceful" was bandied about with increasing contempt by the war party in Germany, whose passions the Crown Prince-- not unwilling to push his royal father prematurely from the pedestal of popularity--was assiduously fanning.

While the fact cannot yet be regarded as established, the writer believes that the future may indubitably show that the Kaiser did have full knowledge of the Austrian ultimatum in advance of its issuance and gave his consent to the policy of that coup in the hope that it would somewhat restore his diminished prestige. He probably followed this policy in the confident expectation that Russia would yield, as it had yielded in 1908 in the Bosnian incident, and when he discovered in Norway that Russia, while willing to maintain peace upon any reasonable terms, was not disposed to surrender all its legitimate interests in the Servian question, he, as will be more fully narrated in the next chapter, hurried back to Berlin and for a time attempted to reverse the policy and bring about a peaceful adjustment.

Unfortunately this attempt came too late. His military camarilla had determined upon war. Preparations were then being feverishly made, and the German and Austrian chancelleries were steadily and deliberately shutting the door upon any possibility of peace.

To withdraw under these circumstances from an untenable position meant a substantial impairment of his already diminished prestige. A Washington would have saved the situation, but the Kaiser was not a Washington.

Another most illuminating feature of this chapter of the Yellow Bookis a report from the French Embassy in Berlin to its Foreign Office on the public opinion of Germany in the summer of 1913, as disclosed by the reports of the French consular representatives in Germany. It gives an extraordinary analysis of conditions in Germany prior to the war, and it describes in great fullness the many causes which were contributory to the creation of a powerful war party in Germany. As it is not in strictness a part of the diplomatic record, it is not embodied in the text of this book, but its value as an acute analysis of conditions in Germany--made before the passions of the war had clouded the judgment--will repay the reader's careful consideration.

The second chapter of the French Yellow Book deals with the events which took place between the murder of the Archduke and the Austrian ultimatum and presents new and cumulative evidence of substantial value.

The French Consul General at Budapest, in a report to his Foreign Office under date July 11, 1914, after showing that the Hungarian Premier, Count Tisza, had refused to disclose, even to the Hungarian Chamber, the results of the judicial inquiry into the Serajevo murder and the decision taken by the Austrian Cabinet, proceeds to show how the suppression of the news in Austria was a part of the scheme to make the ultimatum to Servia so abrupt and speedy that no course would be open to Servia and Europe other than an immediate and unconditional surrender.

Everything is for peace in the newspapers, but the mass of the public believes in war and fears it.... The Government, whether it be seriously desirous of peace, or whether it be preparing a coup, is now doing everything it can to allay this anxiety. That is why the tone of the Government newspapers has been lowered first, by one note and then by two, until now it has become almost optimistic. But the Government newspapers themselves have carefully spread the alarm. Their optimism to order is really without an echo. The nervousness of the Bourse, a barometer one cannot neglect, is a sure proof of that. Stocks, without exception, have fallen to improbably low prices. The Hungarian four per cent. was yesterday quoted at 79.95, a price which has never been quoted since the first issue.[38]

[Footnote 38: French Yellow Book, No. 11.]

Simultaneously a very different note was sounded by the organ of the military party in Vienna. The Milit 鉦 ische Rundschau, a few days before the ultimatum to Servia, said:

"The moment is still favorable for us. If we do not decide upon war, the war we shall have to make in two or three years at the latest will be begun in circumstances much less propitious; now the initiative belongs to us. Russia is not ready, the moral factors are for us, might as well as right. Since some day we shall have to accept the struggle, let us provoke it at once."[39]

[Footnote 39: Ibid., No. 12.]

Before the Austrian ultimatum was issued there had been some preliminary informal negotiations between Austria and Servia and the latter had expressed its willingness to give to Austria the most ample reparation "provided that she did not demand judiciary cooperation," and the Servian Minister at Berlin warned "the German Government that it would be dangerous to endeavor by this inquiry (i.e., by the participation of Austrian officials in the courts of Servia) to damage the prestige of Servia."[40]

[Footnote 40: French Yellow Book, No. 15.]

It thus appears that Austria and Germany had warning in advance of the issuance of the ultimatum that if this humiliating demand were included it would meet with refusal. Their intention to precipitate this war or impose their will upon Europe may therefore be measured by the fact that, with full knowledge that that particular demand would not be accepted, it was made a leading feature of the ultimatum, and finally became the principal outstanding difference after Servia had accepted substantially all the other demands of Austria. This was reported by Cambon to his Foreign Office two days before the ultimatum was issued and at that time Germany was fully advised as to the one demand, which Servia could not in justice to its sovereignty accept. In the same letter, Cambon advises his Foreign Office that Germany had already issued the "preliminary warning of mobilization, which places Germany in a sort of garde-?vous during periods of tension."[41]

[Footnote 41: Ibid., No. 15.]

A further corroboration of Germany's knowledge of the Austrian ultimatum before its issuance is found in a report of the French Minister at Munich to the French Foreign Office, written on the day when the Austrian ultimatum was issued, and a full day before it reached any capital except Berlin and Belgrade. He writes:

The Bavarian Press appears to believe that a peaceful solution of the Austro-Servian incident is not only possible but even probable. Official circles, on the contrary, for some time past, have displayed with more or less sincerity positive pessimism.

The Prime Minister notably said to me to-day that the Austrian note, of which he had cognizance, was in his opinion drawn up in terms acceptable to Servia, but that the present situation appeared to him none the less to be very grave.[42]

[Footnote 42: French Yellow Book, No. 21.]

As it is unlikely that the Austrian Government would have dealt directly with the Bavarian Government without similar communications to the German Foreign Office, it follows as a strong probability that the German Foreign Office and probably each of the constituent States of Germany knew on July the 23d that Austria intended to demand that which Servia had previously indicated its unalterable determination to refuse. Under these circumstances the repeated and insistent assurances that the German Foreign Office gave to England, France, and Russia that it "had no knowledge of the text of the Austrian note before it was handed in and had not exercised any influence on its contents"[43] presents a policy of deception unworthy of a great nation or of the twentieth century.

[Footnote 43: Ante, p. 36.]

It regarded this policy of submarine diplomacy as necessary, not only to throw the other nations off their guard while Germany was arming, but also to support its contention that the quarrel between Servia and Austria was a local quarrel. If it appeared that Germany had instigated Austria in its course, it could not have supported its first contention that the quarrel was a local one and it could not reasonably dispute the right of Russia to intervene. For this purpose the fable was invented. It deceived no one.

The French Yellow Book discloses another even more amazing feature of this policy of deception, for it shows on the authority of the Italian Foreign Minister that Germany and Austria did not even take their own ally into their confidence. The significance of this fact cannot be overestimated. Nothing in the whole record more clearly demonstrates the purpose of the German and Austrian diplomats to set a trap for the rest of Europe.

Under the terms of the Triple Alliance it was the duty of each member to submit to its associates all matters which might involve the possibility of joint cooperation. Even if this had not been written in the very terms of the Alliance, it would follow as a necessary implication, for when each member obligated itself to cooperate with its allies in any attack upon either of them, but not in any aggressive war, it necessarily followed that each ally had the right to the fullest information as to any controversy which might involve such action, so that it might determine whether it fell within the terms of the obligation.

Neither the German nor the Austrian Foreign Office have ever submitted any documentary proof that they discharged this obligation to their ally and it may be added they have never pretended that they did so.

If further proof were needed, we find in the French Yellow Book a report from the French Minister at Rome to his Foreign Office, under date July the 27th, reporting a conversation between the French Minister and the Italian Foreign Minister, the Marquis di San Giuliano, on that day, in which the latter spoke of the

contents of the Austrian note, and assured me that he had had no previous knowledge of them whatever.

He was well aware that the note was to be vigorous and energetic in character, but he had no idea that it could take such a form. I asked him if it was true, as is stated in certain newspapers, that in this connection he had expressed in Vienna approval of Austrian action, and had given the assurance that Italy would fulfill her duties as an ally towards Austria. He replied, "In no way have we been consulted; we have been told nothing whatever. We have therefore had no reason to make any communication of this nature in Vienna."[44]

[Footnote 44: French Yellow Book, No. 72.]

The reason for this secrecy is not far to seek. Almost a year before the Archduke's death, Austria had sounded Italy as to its willingness to acquiesce or participate in a war by Austria against Servia, and Italy had refused. For this reason and also because an Austrian war against Servia was not to the interests of Italy, Austria and Germany both recognized, without even consulting their ally, that they could not count upon its cooperation in such a war. To submit their proposed action to Italy was to invite a deliberate expression of disapproval, and this would make it more difficult for them to demand its cooperation, if they could carry out their policy of so flouting Russia as to compel it to initiate an aggressive war, as they clearly hoped to do.

There was, however, another and very practical reason for this failure to consult their ally. We have seen that the whole policy of the Austrian ultimatum was founded upon secrecy. The plan was to give to Europe no possible intimation of the intended action until it was accomplished and then to give to Europe only twenty-four hours within which to deliberate or act. If as a matter of courtesy Austria and Germany submitted to their ally their proposed course of action, Italy, being wholly opposed to any such unprovoked attack upon Servia, might find a way, either by open and public protest or by dropping a confidential intimation, to advise the other countries as to what was in preparation. This would defeat the principal purpose of Germany and Austria, to force a quick decision and to prepare for eventualities before any other country could make ready. Germany and Austria therefore wholly ignored their ally and pursued their stealthy policy to its discreditable end.

When their diplomatic communications are disclosed in full, this feature of their policy may disclose some significant admissions.

We have already seen (ante, p. 35) that when on July the 20th, three days before the Austrian ultimatum was issued, Sir Edward Grey asked Prince Lichnowsky, the German Ambassador in London, as to what news he had from Vienna with reference to the intentions of his country, Prince Lichnowsky affected to be ignorant. But it appears from a letter, which M. Paul Cambon[45] wrote to his Foreign Office on July the 24th, 1914, that Prince Lichnowsky had returned to London from Berlin about a month before and had "displayed pessimistic views as to the relations between St. Petersburg and Berlin." Cambon adds that the English Foreign Office and his other diplomatic colleagues had all been struck "by the anxious appearance of Prince Lichnowsky since his return from Berlin."[46]

[Footnote 45: The French Ambassador at London.]

[Footnote 46: French Yellow Book, No. 32.]

So designedly was the Austrian ultimatum withheld from the chancelleries of Europe, other than Vienna and Berlin, that on the day following its issuance at Belgrade, the only information which M. Jules Cambon had of its issuance were the extracts in the press, and he thereupon saw the German Secretary of State and asked him whether such an ultimatum had been sent.

Herr von Jagow replied affirmatively, adding that the note was energetic, and that he approved it, the Servian Government having long since exhausted Austrian patience. He considers, moreover, that for Austria the question is one of a domestic nature, and he hopes that it will be localized. I then said to him that, not having received any instructions, I only wished to have with him an entirely personal exchange of views. I then asked him if the Berlin Cabinet had really been in complete ignorance of the Austrian claims before they were communicated to Belgrade, and as he replied that this was so, I expressed my surprise that he should thus undertake to support pretensions, the limit and nature of which he ignored.

"It is only," said Herr von Jagow, interrupting me, "because we are talking personally between ourselves that I allow you to say that to me."

"Certainly," I replied, "but if Peter I. humiliates himself Servia will probably be given over to internal troubles. That will open the door to fresh possibilities, and do you know where Vienna will lead you?" I added that the language of the German Press was not that of a people who were indifferent and foreign to the affair, but told of active support. Finally, I remarked that the shortness of the time given to Servia in which to yield would make a bad impression upon Europe.

Herr von Jagow replied that he expected "un peu d'emotion," on the part of Servia's friends, but that he counted upon their giving Servia good advice.

"I do not doubt," I then said, "that Russia will make an effort in Belgrade to bring the Cabinet to make what concessions are acceptable, but if you ask something of one, why not ask it of the other? And if it be expected that advice will be given in Belgrade, is it not legitimate to expect that on the other hand advice will also be tendered to Vienna?"

The Secretary of State allowed himself to say that that would depend on circumstances, but, recovering himself immediately, declared that the matter must be localized. He asked me if really I considered the situation serious. "Assuredly," I replied, "for, if what is going on has been pondered over, I do not understand why people have cut their bridges behind them."[47]

[Footnote 47: French Yellow Book, No. 30.]

The Yellow Book throws further light upon the extraordinarily petty finesse, with which the chancelleries of Berlin and Vienna attempted to take a snap judgment upon the rest of Europe. We learn from Exhibit No. 55 that Count Berchtold had given to the Russian Ambassador at Vienna, prior to the issuance of the ultimatum, an express assurance "that the claims against Servia would be thoroughly acceptable," and that upon this assurance Count Schebeko had left Vienna on a leave of absence. During his absence and at a time when the President of the French Republic, the French Premier, and its Minister of Foreign Affairs were far distant from Paris and on the high seas, the ultimatum was issued, and, as we have seen, Count Berchtold immediately betook himself to Ischl and remained there until the expiration of the brief time limit in the ultimatum.

The same policy was pursued with reference to other Ambassadors, for when France instructed its representative in Vienna "to call the attention of the Austrian Government to the anxiety aroused in Europe, Baron Macchio stated to our Ambassador that the tone of the Austrian note and the demands formulated by it permitted one to count upon a pacific d 阁 ouement."[48]

[Footnote 48: French Yellow Book, No. 20.]

In the same communication, in which this information is embodied, we gain the important information that "in the Vienna Diplomatic Corps the German Ambassador recommends violent resolutions whilst declaring ostensibly that the Imperial Chancellery is not wholly in agreement with him on this point."

Pursuant to the same ostrich policy, the German Secretary of State, as we have previously seen (ante, pp. 71-75), gave to both the French and English Ambassadors the absence of Count Berchtold at Ischl as an excuse for the failure of Germany to get any extension of the time limit, and not only did he assure them repeatedly and in the most unequivocal way that the German Foreign Office had no knowledge of, or responsibility for, the Austrian ultimatum, but when on July the 25th the Russian Charg?requested a personal appointment with von Jagow in order to present his country's request for such an extension, the German Secretary of State only gave "him an appointment at the end of the afternoon, that is to say, at the moment when the ultimatum will expire," and in view of this illusory appointment the Russian Charg?(M. Bronewsky)

sent, with all speed, a written note to the Secretary of State, in which he pointed out that the delay of the communication made by Austria to the Powers rendered the effect of the communication illusory, since it did not give the Powers time to become acquainted with the facts alleged before the expiry of the ultimatum. He insisted very urgently on the necessity of extending it, if one had not in view the creation of a great crisis.[49]

[Footnote 49: French Yellow Book, No. 42.]

Thus in Berlin and Vienna by concerted action the representatives of England, France, and Russia were evaded until the time limit for Servia had expired.

Contrast with this petty finesse the spirit with which Sazonof attempted to reach an agreement with the Austrian Ambassador at St. Petersburg on July 26th, as set forth in the report of the French Ambassador at St. Petersburg, under that date. He says:

The Minister for Foreign Affairs continues with praiseworthy perseverance to seek means to bring about a peaceful solution. "I shall show myself ready to negotiate up to the last instant," he said to me.

It is in this spirit that he has asked Count[50] to come and see him for a "frank and loyal explanation." In his presence M. Sazonof discussed the Austro-Hungarian ultimatum, article by article, showing clearly the insulting character of the different clauses. "The intention which inspired this document," he said, "is legitimate if you pursue no other aim but the protection of your territory against the agitation of Servian anarchists, but the step to which you have had recourse is not defensible." He concluded, "Take back your ultimatum, modify its form, and I will guarantee the result."[51]

[Footnote 50: The Austrian Ambassador.]

[Footnote 51: French Yellow Book, No. 54.]

Upon one phase of Germany's foreign policy in this crisis the French Yellow Book naturally throws more light than the other publications. I refer to the attempt of Germany to coerce France into a position of neutrality, or possibly to secure from it some definition of its attitude, which would compromise its relations with Russia. The Yellow Book charges that the German Ambassador, under the pretext of securing an authorized statement to the press to allay public excitement, thus attempted to compromise France. The documents go far to suggest this possibility but are not wholly convincing.

The German Ambassador on July the 24th, the very day that the ultimatum reached the chancelleries of Europe, and on the day when von Jagow untruthfully claimed that it had first reached Berlin, called upon the French Minister for Foreign Affairs and read to him a formal note, of which he was unwilling to leave a copy, although he characterized it as a note of importance.

It may be here noted that on more than one occasion in this diplomatic crisis the German representatives were unwilling to leave a copy of the diplomatic messages which they orally communicated.

In his memorandum the French Minister for Foreign Affairs says:

The German Ambassador especially directed my attention to the last two paragraphs of his note before he read it. He indicated that in them lay the chief point. I took note of the actual text, which is as follows: "The German Government considers that the present question is a matter to be settled exclusively between Austria-Hungary and Servia, and that the Powers have the greatest interest in restricting it to the two interested parties. The German Government ardently desires the localization of the conflict, since by the natural play of alliances any intervention by another Power would have incalculable consequences."

I remarked to the German Ambassador that just as it appeared to be legitimate to call for the punishment of all those concerned in the crime of Serajevo, on the other hand it seemed difficult to require measures which could not be accepted, having regard to the dignity and sovereignty of Servia; the Servian Government, even if it was willing to submit to them, would risk being carried away by a revolution.

I also pointed out to Herr von Schoen[52] that his note only took into account two hypotheses: that of a pure and simple refusal or that of a provocative attitude on the part of Servia. The third hypothesis (which would leave the door open for an arrangement) should also be taken into consideration; that of Servia's acceptance and of her agreeing at once to give full satisfaction for the punishment of the accomplices and full guarantees for the suppression of the anti-Austrian propaganda so far as they were compatible with her sovereignty and dignity.

[Footnote 52: The German Ambassador.]

I added that if within these limits the satisfaction desired by Austria could be admitted, the means of obtaining it could be examined; if Servia gave obvious proof of goodwill it could not be thought that Austria would refuse to take part in the conversation.

Perhaps they should not make it too difficult for third party Powers, who could not either morally or sentimentally cease to take interest in Servia, to take an attitude which was in accord with the wishes of Germany to localize the dispute.

Herr von Schoen recognized the justice of these considerations and vaguely stated that hope was always possible. When I asked him if we should give to the Austrian note the character of a simple mise en demeure, which permitted a discussion, or an ultimatum, he answered that personally he had no views.[53]

[Footnote 53: French Yellow Book, No. 28.]

On the following day the German Ambassador again called at the French Foreign Office and protested against an article, which had appeared in a Paris newspaper and which had characterized his communication of the preceding day as the "German menace." The German Ambassador again gave an unequivocal assurance

that there was no agreement between Austria and Germany over the Austrian note, of which the German Government was ignorant, although the German Government had subsequently approved it on receiving communication of it at the same time as the other Powers.[54]

[Footnote 54: Ibid., No. 36.]

The hardihood of this statement, in view of the fact that on the preceding day, simultaneously with the service of the ultimatum, the threatening demand had been delivered by Germany to the leading European chancelleries that the quarrel between Austria and Servia must be localized, is apparent. Baron von Schoen, the German Ambassador, then denied that his suggestion of "incalculable consequences," if the dispute were not localized, was a "menace." This statement, repeated by German diplomats in other capitals, approaches the ludicrous. The first military power of Europe formally advises other nations that unless they waive their legitimate claims and interests, "incalculable consequences" will follow, and it is gravely suggested that this is not a "menace."

On the following day Baron von Schoen made two visits at the French Foreign Office and assured the acting Minister for Foreign Affairs that

Germany was on the side of France in the ardent desire for the maintenance of peace, and she earnestly hoped that France would use her influence in a soothing manner in St. Petersburg.

I replied to this suggestion that Russia was moderate, that she had committed no act throwing doubt upon her moderation, and that we were in agreement with her in seeking for a peaceful solution of the struggle. It therefore appeared to me that in counterpart Germany should act in Vienna, where the efficacy of her action was sure, with a view to avoiding military operations tending to the occupation of Servia.

The Ambassador having pointed out to me that that was irreconcilable with the position adopted by Germany, "that the question only concerned Austria and Servia," I said to him that mediation in Vienna and St. Petersburg might be made by the four Powers who were less directly interested in the matter.

Baron von Schoen then sheltered himself behind his lack of instructions on this point, and I told him that in these circumstances I did not feel able to act in St. Petersburg alone.

Our conversation concluded with the renewed assurance by the Ambassador as to the peaceful intentions of Germany, who, he declared, was with France on this point.[55]

[Footnote 55: French Yellow Book, No. 56.]

The incident now followed, which suggested to the French Foreign office a subtle attempt of Germany to compromise the relations of France with Russia by imputing disloyalty to the former. On his second visit a few hours later,

Baron von Schoen desired the French Foreign Office to give to the public a statement with reference to the preceding interview, and suggested the following, which he dictated to the French official:

"The German Ambassador and the Minister of Foreign Affairs had a further interview in the course of the afternoon, during which they examined, in the most friendly spirit and with a feeling of pacific solidarity, the means which might be employed for the maintenance of general peace."

The Acting Political Director at once replied: "Then, in your mind, everything is settled, and you give us the assurance that Austria accepts the Servian note, or will be willing to converse with the Powers with regard to it?"

The Ambassador appeared to be taken aback, and made a vigorous denial. It was therefore pointed out to him that if nothing had changed in the negative attitude of Germany, the terms of the suggested "note to the Press" were excessive, and likely to give French opinion a false feeling of security by creating illusions as to the actual situation, the dangers of which were but too evident.[56]

[Footnote 56: French Yellow Book, No. 57.]

It is not surprising that the French Foreign Office looked askance at these German suggestions of "pacific solidarity" with France, which contrasted so strangely with Germany's refusal to work for peace and its sinister menaces to other countries. France's suspicion that Baron von Schoen was thus attempting to compromise its loyalty in the eyes of Russia cannot be said to be without some foundation, although it is as reasonable to assume that these professions of the German Ambassador were only an incident to the general plan of lulling France and its allies into a false sense of security. Here again the full truth can only be ascertained when Germany is willing to submit to the scrutiny of the world the records of its Foreign Office.

On July 26th, M. Jules Cambon had an interview with the German Secretary of State and earnestly supported Sir Edward Grey's suggestion that a conference be called in which England, France, Germany, and Italy should participate for the preservation of peace. This interview is at once so dramatic, and almost prophetic, that it justifies quotation in extenso:

To Cambon's proposition, von Jagow replied, as he did to the British Ambassador, that he could not accept a proposal to charge the Italian, French, and German Ambassadors with the task of seeking, with Sir Edward Grey, a means of solving the present difficulties, for that would be to establish a regular conference to deal with the affairs of Austria and Russia. I replied to Herr von Jagow that I regretted his response, but that the great object, which Sir Edward Grey had in view, was above a question of form, and what was important was the association of England and France with Germany and Italy in laboring for peace; that this association could show itself in common action in St. Petersburg and Vienna; that he had frequently expressed to me his regret at seeing the two groups of alliances always opposed to each other in Europe, and that here he had an opportunity of proving that there was a European spirit, by showing four Powers belonging to the two groups acting in common agreement to prevent a struggle. Herr von Jagow evaded the matter by saying that Germany had her engagements with Austria. I pointed out that the relations of Germany with Vienna were no more close than those of France with Russia, and that it was he himself who raised the question of the two opposed groups of alliances.

The Secretary of State then said that he did not refuse to act with a view to avoiding an Austro-Russian conflict, but that he could not intervene in the Austro-Servian conflict. "One is the consequence of the other," I said, "and it would be well to prevent the creation of any new state of affairs calculated to bring about the intervention of Russia."

As the Secretary of State persisted in saying that he was obliged to observe his engagements with regard to Austria, I asked him if he had pledged himself to follow Austria everywhere blindfold, and if he had made himself acquainted with the Servian reply to Austria, which had been handed to him that morning by the Servian Charg?d'Affaires. "I have not yet had time," he said. "I regret it," I replied. "You will see that except on points of detail Servia has yielded completely. It would seem, however, that since Austria has obtained the satisfaction, which your support procured her, you might to-day advise her to be content, or to examine with Servia the terms of the Servian reply."

As Herr von Jagow did not answer me clearly, I asked him if Germany wanted war. He protested energetically, saying that he knew that that was my idea but that it was completely incorrect. "You must then," I replied, "act in consequence. When you read the Servian reply, weigh the terms with your conscience, I beg you in the name of humanity, and do not personally assume a portion of the responsibility for the catastrophe, whose preparation you are allowing." Herr von Jagow protested again, adding that he was ready to join England and France in any common effort, but that some form must be found for this intervention which he could accept and that the Cabinets should agree among themselves upon the matter. "Moreover," he added, "direct conversations between Vienna and St. Petersburg are begun and are proceeding. I expect much good of them, and I have hope."[57]

[Footnote 57: French Yellow Book, No. 74.]

In his solemn injunction to von Jagow "in the name of humanity" to weigh the terms in his conscience, Cambon struck a loftier note than any of the diplomatic disputants. Macaulay has said that the "French mind has always been the interpreter between national ideas and those of universal mankind," and at least since the French Revolution the tribute has been deserved.

He, who carefully and dispassionately reads the diplomatic correspondence which preceded the war, must be impressed with the different point of view of the two groups of disputants. Both the written and oral communications of the German and Austrian representatives failed to suggest at any time a note other than one of selfish nationalism. We search in vain for the most distant recognition of the fact that the world at large had any legitimate interest in the controversy. The insistent note, which Austria sounded, was that its interests required its punitive action against Servia, even though the peace of the world were thereby sacrificed, and that of Germany repeated with equal insistence that its "closest interests" summoned it to the side of Austria.

In marked contrast to this spirit of national selfishness is the repeated admonition of Sir Edward Grey that the whole question should be considered in its "larger aspects," thereby meaning the peace and welfare of Europe; while the Czar, with evident sincerity, suggested to the Kaiser that "with the aid of God it must be possible to our long tried friendship to prevent the shedding of blood," and proposed a reference of the question to the Hague.

Similarly the appeal of Jules Cambon to von Jagow, "in the name of humanity" was more than the ordinary exchange of diplomatic views. Von Jagow's conception of his duty is shown by the fact that he had taken a position involving "incalculable consequences" without even reading the Servian reply.

Cambon approved himself a worthy "yoke fellow in equity" with Sir Edward Grey, and no loftier tone was sounded by any participant in this great controversy, unless we except Goschen's solemn statement to von Bethmann-Hollweg in the equally dramatic interview, which succeeded the rupture of relations between England and Germany, when Goschen stated that "it was so to speak a matter of life and death for the honor of Great Britain that she should keep her solemn engagement to do her utmost to defend Belgium's neutrality if attacked," and added, "that fear of consequences could hardly be regarded as an excuse for breaking solemn promises."

CHAPTER VIII

THE INTERVENTION OF THE KAISER

The Kaiser now appears upon the scene with a fatal result to the peace of Europe. One fact in this controversy is too clear for dispute. When peace proposals were still under consideration and some slight progress had been made by the eleventh-hour consent of Austria on July 31 to discuss with Russia the merits of the Servian question, the Kaiser--like Brennus with his v?victis--threw his sword into the trembling scales and definitely turned the balance against the peace of the world.

Was it a reluctant Caesar who thus crossed the Rubicon, at whose fateful margin he had stood at other crises of his peaceful reign without destroying that peace?

Our information is still too meager to justify a satisfactory answer at this time. Not only are the premises in dispute, but the inferences from admitted premises are too conflicting.

At the time the Austrian Archduke was murdered the Kaiser was in Berlin, and he at once showed an intense interest in the event and in all that it portended. It was officially announced that he planned to attend the funeral in Vienna, but later the world was advised that he had suffered a "chill," which would prevent such attendance. Perhaps it was a diplomatic chill. He then left for Norway, where he remained in the enjoyment of his annual holiday until the evening of July 26th, when he suddenly returned to his Capitol.

Evidently his return was unexpected, for we learn from a telegram from Sir H. Rumbold to Sir Edward Grey, dated July 26th, that,

the Emperor returned suddenly to-night and [the German] Under-Secretary of State for Foreign Affairs says that the Foreign Office regrets this step which was taken on His Majesty's own initiative. They fear that His Majesty's sudden return may cause speculation and excitement.

As the refusal of Austria to accept the Servian reply and its severance of all diplomatic relations with that country had already thrown the entire world into a state of feverish anxiety, it is difficult to understand why the German Foreign Office should have felt that the very natural return of the Kaiser to his Capitol at one of the greatest crises in the history of his country and of the world should be regarded as giving rise to "speculation and excitement," especially as the President of the French Republic was hastening back to Paris.

The Under-Secretary of State's deprecation of the Kaiser's return suggests the possibility that the German Foreign Office, which had already made substantial progress in precipitating the crisis, did not wish the Kaiser's return for fear that he might again exert, as in the Moroccan crisis, his great influence in the interests of peace.

It felt that it had the matter well in hand, but never before did a foreign office blunder so flagrantly and with such disastrous results. From beginning to end every anticipation that the German Chancellor had was falsified by events. This discreditable and blundering chapter of German diplomacy is enough to make the bones of the sagacious Bismarck turn in his grave.

As appears from Sir M. de Bunsen's dispatch to Sir Edward Grey, dated July 26th, it was the confident belief of the German diplomats that "Russia will keep quiet during the chastisement of Servia," and that "France too was not at all in a position for facing the war."[58]

[Footnote 58: English White Paper, No. 32.]

When the full history of this imbroglio is written, it will probably be found that the extensive labor troubles in St. Petersburg, the military unpreparedness of Russia and France, and the political schism in England, then verging to civil war, had deeply impressed both Vienna and Berlin that the dual alliance could impose its will upon Europe with reference to Servia without any serious risk of a European war.

While for these reasons Germany and Austria may not have regarded such a war or the intervention of England therein as probable, yet the dual alliance recognized from the outset such a possibility. The uncertainty as to the Kaiser's attitude with respect to such a war may therefore explain the "regret," with which the German Foreign Office witnessed his sudden and uninvited return.

On his return the diplomatic negotiations, which had commenced with an allegro con brio, for a time changed under the baton of the Imperial Conductor into a more peaceful andante, until the Kaiser made one of his characteristically sudden changes of purpose and precipitated the war by an arrogant ultimatum to Russia, which that country could not possibly accept without a fatal sacrifice of its self-respect and prestige as a nation.

If it be true--and the future may demonstrate it--that this war was planned by Germany at least as far back as the Moroccan crisis, then the Kaiser's responsibility for the commencement of the quarrel cannot be doubted. It is inconceivable that the German Foreign Office could pursue for three years the policy of precipitating a European war without the knowledge and consent of the "Over War Lord."

When full data are accessible as to the importations by Germany in advance of the war, as to its withdrawal of foreign credits and placing of foreign loans, its sales of stocks by influential investors, and its importations on the eve of the war of horses and foodstuffs, a strong circumstantial case may be developed of a deliberate purpose to retrieve the Moroccan fiasco by an audacious coup which would determine the mastery of Europe. The levy in 1913 of an extraordinary tax upon capital, which virtually confiscated the earnings of the German people for military purposes, adds much support to this contention. According to Giolitti, the former Italian Premier, Austria sounded Italy in August, 1913, as to its willingness to participate in a war against Servia.[59]

[Footnote 59: Giolitti Speech, Italian Chamber, Dec. 5, 1914.]

The inferences to be drawn from the Kaiser's personality are somewhat conflicting. Like all self-centered and highly neurotic personalities, his nature is essentially a dual one. This does not mean that he is in any sense a hypocrite, for one of the engaging features of his attractive personality has been the candor and sincerity which have marked nearly all his public acts. He has shown himself to be a man of opposite moods, and conflicting purposes, having almost as many public poses as he has costumes, and a strong desire to play as many varied roles as possible on the stage of the world. Like Bottom in the Midsummer Night's Dream, he would play all parts from the "roaring lion" to the shrinking Thisbe.

The ruler who sent a sympathetic message to Kruger as an insult to England is he who shortly thereafter gratuitously submitted to Queen Victoria military plans for the subjugation of the Boers.

The ruler, who sent the Panther to Agadir, later restrained his country from declaring war against England, when Lloyd George threw down the gauntlet in his Mansion House speech in the Moroccan crisis.

As preacher, the Kaiser exalted within sight of the Mount of Olives the precepts of Christian humility, and yet advised his soldiers, on their departure to China, to "take no prisoners and give no quarter." The most affable and democratic monarch on occasion will in another mood assume the outworn toggery of medi 鑾 al absolutism. A democratic business monarch, and as such the advance agent of German prosperity, he yet shocks the common sense and awakens the ridicule of the world by posing as a combination of Caesar and Mahomet.

The avowed champion of Christianity, who has preached with the fervor of

Peter the Hermit against the Yellow Race, he has nevertheless, since this war began, instigated the Sultan of Turkey to proclaim in the Moslem world a "holy war" against his Christian enemies.

Pacific and bellicose by turns the monarch, who throughout his whole reign has hitherto kept the peace of the world, has yet on slight pretext given utterance to the most warlike and incendiary statements.

How is it possible to draw any inference from such a personality, of whom it could be said, as Sydney Smith once said of Lord John Russell, that

there is nothing he would not undertake. I believe he would perform an operation for stone, build St. Peter's, assume (with or without ten minutes' notice) the command of the Channel Fleet, and no one would discover from his manner that the patient had died, that St. Peter's had tumbled down, and that the Channel Fleet had been knocked to atoms.

We should therefore dismiss all inferences suggested by his complex personality and should judge him by what he did from the time that he suddenly arrived in Berlin on July 26th, until the issuance by his direct order of the fatal ultimatum to Russia.

Before proceeding to analyze the very interesting and dramatic correspondence, which passed between the rulers of Germany, England, and Russia--doubly interesting because of the family relationship and the unusual personal and cousinly intimacy of these dispatches--it is well to inquire what the Kaiser could have done that would have immediately avoided the crisis and saved the situation. So far as the published record goes, he did not send a single telegram in the interests of peace to his illustrious ally, the Emperor Francis Joseph.

Let us suppose that he had sent the following:

I have just returned to Berlin and find Europe on the verge of war. I sympathize entirely with you and your country in its demands upon Servia. I agree with you that the Servian reply is not satisfactory. In accordance with the obligations of our alliance, I shall in any event support with the full power of the German sword the cause of Austria. Servia has by its reply admitted its responsibility for the murder of the Archduke and has unreservedly accepted certain of your demands, and as to others has agreed to submit them either to The Hague Tribunal for arbitration, or to a concert of Powers. You will decide whether Austria is satisfied to accept either of these suggestions, but as England, France, and Russia have asked that time be granted to consider a peaceful and satisfactory solution of the difficulty, and as the questions reserved by Servia can be used as the basis for further discussion without prejudice to the rights of Austria, and as it is to the interest of every country and the entire world that its peace should not be broken unnecessarily, I shall be gratified if you can agree that a reasonable time shall be granted as a matter of courtesy to Russia, England, and France, in order that it may be determined upon due consideration whether it is not possible to preserve peace without sacrificing in any respect the legitimate demands of Austria, which have my full sympathy and support.

WILHELM.

Would the Austrian Emperor, himself a noble-minded and peace-loving monarch, have refused this reasonable request? A little time, a little patience and some forbearance for the rights of other States and the youth of Europe need not have perished. Again, "the pity of it."

In its place the following correspondence took place between the Kaiser on the one hand and the Czar and King George on the other. It is so dramatic that it justifies quotation in extenso.

On the night of July 28th, the Kaiser sent the following dispatch to the Czar:

I have heard with the greatest anxiety of the impression which is caused by the action of Austria-Hungary against Servia. The unscrupulous agitation which has been going on for years in Servia has led to the revolting crime of which Archduke Franz Ferdinand has become a victim. The spirit which made the Servians murder their own King and his consort still dominates that country. Doubtless You will agree with me that both of us, You as well as I, and all other sovereigns, have a common interest to insist that all those who are responsible for this horrible murder shall suffer their deserved punishment.

On the other hand I by no means overlook the difficulty encountered by You and Your Government to stem the tide of public opinion. In view of the cordial friendship which has joined us both for a long time with firm ties, I shall use my entire influence to induce Austria-Hungary to obtain a frank and satisfactory understanding with Russia. I hope confidently that You will support me in my efforts to overcome all difficulties which may yet arise.[60]

[Footnote 60: German White Paper, No. 20. The Capitals to the pronouns follow the original correspondence.]

This telegram rings true, and fairly suggests a pacific attitude on the part of the Kaiser when he first took the helm on his return from Norway. Its weakness lies in the fact that the record, as presented by the German Government, does not disclose any communication which he sent to his Austrian ally in the interests of peace. We have the frequent assurances of the Kaiser to the Czar that he was exerting all his influence to induce his ally to come to a satisfactory understanding with Russia, but neither over the signature of the Kaiser nor over that of his Foreign Minister does the record show a single communication addressed to Vienna in the interests of peace.

The Czar did not fail to appreciate this, and his reply to the Kaiser rings quite as true and suggests the crux of the whole problem. It reads:

I am glad that You are back in Germany. In this serious moment I ask You earnestly to help me. An ignominious war has been declared against a weak country, and in Russia the indignation, which I fully share, is tremendous. I fear that very soon I shall be unable to resist the pressure exercised upon me and that I shall be forced to take measures which will lead to war. To prevent such a calamity as a European war would be, I urge You in the name of our old friendship to do all in Your power to restrain Your ally from going too far.[61]

[Footnote 61: German White Paper, No. 21.]

Who can deny the force of the sentence thus italicized? It was Austria which was the provocative factor. It was then bombarding Belgrade and endeavoring to cross the Danube into Servia. It had declared war, and brusquely refused even to discuss the question with Russia. It was mobilizing its army, and making every effort to make a speedy subjugation of Servia. If peace was to be preserved, the pressure must begin with Austria. If any question remained for peace parleys, the status quo must be preserved. Russia could not permit Austria to destroy Servia first and then discuss its justice.

Thereupon the Kaiser telegraphed the Czar as follows:

I have received Your telegram and I share Your desire for the conservation of peace. However I cannot--as I told You in my first telegram--consider the action of Austria-Hungary as an "ignominious war." Austria-Hungary knows from experience that the promises of Servia as long as they are merely on paper are entirely unreliable.

According to my opinion the action of Austria-Hungary is to be considered as an attempt to receive full guaranty that the promises of Servia are effectively translated into deeds. In this opinion I am strengthened by the explanation of the Austrian Cabinet that Austria-Hungary intended no territorial gain at the expense of Servia. I am therefore of opinion that it is perfectly possible for Russia to remain a spectator in the Austro-Servian war without drawing Europe into the most terrible war it has ever seen. I believe that a direct understanding is possible and desirable between Your Government and Vienna, an understanding which--as I have already telegraphed You--my Government endeavors to aid with all possible effort. Naturally military measures by Russia, which might be construed as a menace by Austria-Hungary, would accelerate a calamity which both of us desire to avoid and would undermine my position as mediator which--upon Your appeal to my friendship and aid--I willingly accepted.[62]

[Footnote 62: German White Paper, No. 22. See note, post., p. 189.]

The Kaiser's fatal error lies in the concluding paragraph of this telegram, in claiming that Russia should not take any military measures pending the Kaiser's mediation, although Austria should be left free not merely to make such preparations against Russia, but to pursue its aggressive war then already commenced against Servia. If the belligerents were expected to desist from military preparations, should not the obligation be reciprocal?

Later that night the Kaiser again telegraphed the Czar:

My Ambassador has instructions to direct the attention of Your Government to the dangers and serious consequences of a mobilization; I have told You the same in my last telegram. Austria-Hungary has mobilized only against Servia, and only a part of her army. If Russia, as seems to be the case according to Your advice and that of Your Government, mobilizes against Austria-Hungary, the part of the mediator, with which You have entrusted me in such friendly manner and which I have accepted upon Your express desire, is threatened if not made impossible. The entire weight of decision now rests upon Your shoulders. You have to bear the responsibility for war or peace.[63]

[Footnote 63: German White Paper, No. 23.]

To which the Czar replied as follows:

I thank You from my heart for Your quick reply. I am sending to-night Tatisheff (Russian honorary aide to the Kaiser) with instructions. The military measures now taking form were decided upon five days ago, and for the reason of defense against the preparations of Austria. I hope with all my heart that these measures will not influence in any manner Your position as mediator which I appraise very highly. We need Your strong pressure upon Austria so that an understanding can be arrived at with us.[64]

[Footnote 64: German White Paper, No. 23 A.]

Later the Czar again telegraphed the Kaiser:

I thank You cordially for Your mediation which permits the hope that everything may yet end peaceably. It is technically impossible to discontinue our military preparations which have been made necessary by the Austrian mobilization. It is far from us to want war. As long as the negotiations between Austria and Servia continue, my troops will undertake no provocative action. I give You my solemn word thereon. I confide with all my faith in the grace of God, and I hope for the success of Your mediation in Vienna for the welfare of our countries and the peace of Europe.

What more could the Kaiser reasonably ask? Here was an assurance from the ruler of a great nation, and his royal cousin, that on his "solemn word" no provocative action would be taken by Russia "as long as the negotiations between Austria and Servia continue" and this notwithstanding the fact that Austria had flouted and ignored Russia, had declared war against Servia and was then endeavoring to subjugate it quickly by bombarding its capital and invading its territory with superior forces.

It is true that the Czar did not order demobilization, and apart from his unquestioned right to prepare for eventualities in the event of the failure of the peace parleys, the Kaiser himself recognized in a later telegram that in the case of Germany when mobilization had once been started it could not be immediately arrested.

Simultaneously King George had telegraphed the Kaiser through Prince Henry as follows:

Thanks for Your telegram; so pleased to hear of William's efforts to concert with Nicky to maintain peace. Indeed I am earnestly desirous that such an irreparable disaster as a European war should be averted. My Government is doing its utmost suggesting to Russia and France to suspend further military preparations if Austria will consent to be satisfied with occupation of Belgrade and neighboring Servian territory as a hostage for satisfactory settlement of her demands; other countries meanwhile suspending their war preparations. Trust William will use his great influence to induce Austria to accept this proposal, thus proving that Germany and England are working together to prevent what would be an international catastrophe. Pray assure William I am doing and shall continue to do all that lies in my power to preserve peace of Europe.[65]

[Footnote 65: Second German White Paper.]

The fairness of this proposal can hardly be disputed. It conceded to Austria the right to occupy the capital of Servia and hold it as a hostage for a satisfactory adjustment of her demands and even to continue her military preparations, while all other nations, including Russia, were to suspend their military preparations. As the Kaiser precipitated the war because Russia would not cease its preparations for eventualities, King George's proposal, upon which neither the Kaiser nor his government ever acted, fully met his demands.

To this the Kaiser replied on July 31st:

Many thanks for kind telegram. Your proposals coincide with My ideas and with the statements I got this night from Vienna which I have had forwarded to London. I just received news from Chancellor that official notification has just reached him that this night Nicky has ordered the mobilization of his whole army and fleet. He has not even awaited the results of the mediation I am working at, and left Me without any news. I am off for Berlin to take measures for ensuring safety of My eastern frontiers where strong Russian troops are already posted.[66]

[Footnote 66: Second German White Paper.]

On its face this reply seems not unreasonable, but it must not be forgotten that Austria continued not only to bombard Belgrade but to mobilize its armies against Russia as well as Servia. Russia agreed to stop all military preparations, if Austria would consent to discuss the Servian question with a view to peace. Austria until the eleventh hour--when it was too late--refused even to discuss the Servian question and never offered either to demobilize or to cease its attack upon Servia. Germany upheld her in this unwarrantable course.

While in principle the Kaiser agreed with the King as to the method of adjustment, there is nothing in the record to indicate that the Kaiser ever made any suggestion to his ally that it should stop its operations against Servia after capturing Belgrade, and await the adjustment of the questions through diplomatic channels.

Thereupon King George sent a brief telegram, stating that he had sent an urgent telegram to the Czar urging this course. Later on July 31st the Kaiser sent the following telegram to the Czar:

Upon Your appeal to my friendship and Your request for my aid I have engaged in mediation between Your Government and the Government of Austria-Hungary. While this action was taking place, Your troops were being mobilized against my ally, Austria-Hungary, whereby, as I have already communicated to You, my mediation has become almost illusory. In spite of this, I have continued it, and now I receive reliable news that serious preparations for war are going on on my eastern frontier. The responsibility for the security of my country forces me to measures of defense. I have gone to the extreme limit of the possible in my efforts for the preservation of the peace of the world. It is not I who bear the responsibility for the misfortune which now threatens the entire civilized world. It rests in Your hand to avert it. No one threatens the honor and peace of Russia which might well have awaited the success of my mediation. The friendship for You and Your country, bequeathed to me by my grandfather on his death-bed, has always been sacred to me, and I have stood faithfully by Russia while it was in serious affliction, especially during its last war. The peace of Europe can still be preserved by You if Russia decides to discontinue those military preparations which menace Germany and Austria-Hungary.

In this fair-spoken message we unhappily find no suggestion that Austria would stop its mobilization, or its military operations against Servia. The untenable position of the Kaiser, to which he adhered with fatal consistency to the end, was that Austria should be given the full right to mobilize against Russia as well as Servia, and that his ally should even be permitted to press its aggressive operations against Servia by taking possession of its capital and holding it as a ransom. In the meantime Russia should not make any military preparations, either to move effectually against Austria in the event of the failure of negotiations, or even to defend itself.

The Kaiser's suggestion did not even carry with it the implication that Germany would stop the military preparations that it was then carrying on in feverish haste, so that the contention of the Kaiser, however plausibly it was veiled in his telegram, was that Germany and Austria should have full freedom to prepare for war against Russia, while Russia was to tie its hands and await the outcome of further parleys, with Austrian cannon bombarding Belgrade.

In this correspondence the Kaiser displayed his recognized ability as a writer and speaker, for in this rapid-fire exchange of telegrams the Kaiser was easily the better controversialist.

He assumed the role of a disinterested party, who, at the request of a litigant, agrees to become an impartial mediator. He was neither. The Czar had not asked him to be a mediator, although in the later telegrams the Russian monarch accepted that term. The Czar in his first telegram had asked the Kaiser as a party to the quarrel "to restrain your ally from going too far." The Kaiser, having adroitly accepted a very different role, promptly shifts the responsibility upon the Czar of embarrassing the so-called "mediation." This enabled him to assume the attitude of "injured innocence" and very skillfully he played that part.

This at least is clear that in this correspondence the Kaiser was either guilty of insincerity or he betrayed a fatal incapacity to grasp the essentials of the quarrel. I prefer the latter construction of his conduct. Against the bellicose efforts of his Foreign Office and his General Staff, I believe that for dynastic reasons he strove for a time to adjust the difficulty, but his egomania and his life-long habit of personal absolutism blinded him to the fact that he was taking an untenable, indeed an impossible, position, in contending that Russia should effectually tie its hands while Germany and Austria should be left free to prepare for eventualities. Had there been a breathing spell and the Kaiser had had more time for reflection, possibly the unreasonableness of his contention would have suggested itself, but he found on his sudden return from Norway that his country, through the fatuous folly of its military party, was almost irrevocably committed to war. Probably he did not dare to reverse openly and formally its policy. His popularity had already suffered in the Moroccan crisis. This consideration and the histrionic side to his complex personality betrayed him into his untenable and fatal position.

The Kaiser has hitherto been regarded as a man of exceptional ability. Time and the issue of this war will tell. The verdict of history may be to the contrary. The world for a time may easily confuse restless energy and habitual meddling with real ability, but its final verdict will go far deeper. Since the Kaiser dropped his sagacious pilot, Germany's real position in the world has steadily weakened. Then it was the first power in Europe with its rivals disunited. The Kaiser has united his enemies with "hoops of steel," driven Russia and England into a close alliance, forced Italy out of the Triple Alliance, and as the only compensation for these disastrous results, he has gained the doubtful cooperation of moribund Turkey, of which he is likely to say before many months are over: "Who shall deliver me from the body of this death?"

In the meantime, Germany was not idle in its preparations for eventualities.

The Kaiser and his counsellors were already definitely planning for the war, and were taking steps to alienate England from her Allies and secure her neutrality. To insure this, the German Chancellor, having visited the Kaiser at Potsdam, sent for the British Ambassador, and made the following significant offer:

[67]I was asked to call upon the Chancellor to-night. His Excellency had just returned from Potsdam.

[Footnote 67: Sir E. Goschen.]

He said that should Austria be attacked by Russia a European conflagration might, he feared, become inevitable, owing to Germany's obligations as Austria's ally, in spite of his continued efforts to maintain peace. He then proceeded to make the following strong bid for British neutrality. He said that it was clear, so far as he was able to judge the main principle which governed British policy, that Great Britain would never stand by and allow France to be crushed in any conflict there might be. That, however, was not the object at which Germany aimed. Provided that neutrality of Great Britain were certain, every assurance would be given to the British Government that the Imperial Government aimed at no territorial acquisitions at the expense of France, should they prove victorious in any war that might ensue.

I questioned his Excellency about the French colonies, and he said that he was unable to give a similar undertaking in that respect. As regards Holland, however, his Excellency said that, so long as Germany's adversaries respected the integrity and neutrality of the Netherlands, Germany was ready to give his Majesty's Government an assurance that she would do likewise. It depended upon the action of France what operations Germany might be forced to enter upon in Belgium, but when the war was over Belgian integrity would be respected if she had not sided against Germany.

His Excellency ended by saying that ever since he had been Chancellor the object of his policy had been, as you were aware, to bring about an understanding with England; he trusted that these assurances might form the basis of that understanding which he so much desired. He had in mind a general neutrality agreement between England and Germany, though it was, of course, at the present moment too early to discuss details, and an assurance of British neutrality in the conflict which the present crisis might possibly produce, would enable him to look forward to a realization of his desire.

In reply to his Excellency's inquiry how I thought his request would appeal to you, I said that I did not think it probable that at this stage of events you would care to bind yourself to any course of action and that I was of opinion that you would desire to retain full liberty.[68]

[Footnote 68: English White Paper, No. 85.]

While the German Foreign Office was thus endeavoring to keep England neutral, its army was on the move against France. This does not rest upon vague allegation, but upon the detailed specifications in a communication from the French Foreign Office, which the French Ambassador in London submitted to Sir Edward Grey on July 31st. Its significance is apparent when it is remembered that simultaneously the Kaiser was invoking the Czar to demobilize his armies, and cease military preparations.

The German army had its advance posts on our frontiers yesterday (Friday). German patrols twice penetrated on to our territory. Our advance posts are withdrawn to a distance of 10 kilometers from the frontier. The local population is protesting against being thus abandoned to the attack of the enemy's army, but the Government wishes to make it clear to public opinion and to the British Government that in no case will France be the aggressor. The whole 16th Corps from Metz, reinforced by a part of the 8th from Treves and Cologne, is occupying the frontier at Metz on the Luxemburg side. The 15th Army Corps from Strassburg has closed up on the frontier. The inhabitants of Alsace-Lorraine are prevented by the threat of being shot from crossing the frontier. Reservists have been called back to Germany by tens of thousands. This is the last stage before mobilization, whereas we have not called out a single reservist.

As you see, Germany has done it. I would add that all my information goes to show that the German preparations began on Saturday, the very day on which the Austrian note was handed in.[69]

In reply to the suggestion of the German Chancellor as to the neutrality of England, Sir Edward Grey advised the English Ambassador on July 30th, as follows:

His Majesty's Government cannot for a moment entertain the Chancellor's proposal that they should bind themselves to neutrality on such terms.

What he asks us in effect is to engage to stand by while French colonies are taken and France is beaten so long as Germany does not take French territory as distinct from the colonies.

From the material point of view such a proposal is unacceptable, for France, without further territory in Europe being taken from her, could be so crushed as to lose her position as a great Power, and become subordinate to German policy.

Altogether apart from that, it would be a disgrace for us to make this bargain with Germany at the expense of France, a disgrace from which the good name of this country would never recover.

The Chancellor also in effect asks us to bargain away whatever obligations or interest we have as regards the neutrality of Belgium. We could not entertain that bargain either.

Having said so much, it is unnecessary to examine whether the prospect of a future general neutrality agreement between England and Germany offered positive advantages sufficient to compensate us for tying our hands now. We must preserve our full freedom to act as circumstances may seem to us to require in any such unfavorable and regrettable development of the present crisis as the Chancellor contemplates.

You should speak to the Chancellor in the above sense, and add most earnestly that one way of maintaining good relations between England and

Germany is that they should continue to work together to preserve the peace of Europe; if we succeed in this object, the mutual relations of Germany and England will, I believe, be ipso facto improved and strengthened. For that object His Majesty's Government will work in that way with all sincerity and goodwill.

And I will say this: If the peace of Europe can be preserved, and the present crisis safely passed, my own endeavor will be to promote some arrangement, to which Germany could be a party, by which she could be assured that no aggressive or hostile policy would be pursued against her or her allies by France, Russia, and ourselves, jointly or separately.

This letter will give Sir Edward Grey lasting glory in the history of civilization. Its chivalrous fairness to France needs no comment, but its most significant feature is the concluding portion, in which the English Foreign Minister suggested to Germany that if peace could be preserved, England stood ready to join with Germany in an alliance which would have insured all the great European nations against any aggressive war on the part of either of them.

It was, in fact, the "United States of Europe" in embryo. It was the one solution possible for these long-continued European wars--essentially civil wars,--namely an alliance by the six great Powers,--a merger of the Triple Alliance and the Triple Entente,--whereby any aggressive act on the part of any one of them would be prevented by the others. What an infinite pity that the imprudent act of the Kaiser, and the mad folly of his advisers probably made a fair trial of this most hopeful plan for the unification of Europe an impossibility for another century!

In order that Germany should have no excuse whatever to declare war on account of Russia's preparations, the Russian Foreign Minister saw the German Ambassador in St. Petersburg on July 30th, and then offered on behalf of Russia to stop all military preparations, provided that Austria would simply recognize as an abstract principle that the Servian question had assumed the character of a question of European interest. As this proposal fully met the demands of the Kaiser with respect to the cessation by Russia of military preparations, the conversation as reported by the English Ambassador at St. Petersburg to Sir Edward Grey on July 30th deserves quotation in extenso:

French Ambassador and I visited Minister for Foreign Affairs this morning. His Excellency said that German Ambassador had told him yesterday afternoon that German Government were willing to guarantee that Servian integrity would be respected by Austria. To this he had replied that this might be so, but nevertheless Servia would become an Austrian vassal, just as, in similar circumstances, Bokhara had become a Russian vassal. There would be a revolution in Russia if she were to tolerate such a state of affairs.

M. Sazonof told us that absolute proof was in possession of Russian Government, that Germany was making military and naval preparations against Russia--more particularly in the direction of the Gulf of Finland.

German Ambassador had a second interview with Minister for Foreign Affairs at 2 A.M., when former completely broke down on seeing that war was inevitable. He appealed to M. Sazonof to make some suggestion which he could telegraph to German Government as a last hope. M. Sazonof accordingly drew up and handed to German Ambassador a formula in French, of which the following is a translation:

"If Austria, recognizing that her conflict with Servia has assumed character of question of European interest, declares herself ready to eliminate from her ultimatum points which violate principle of sovereignty of Servia, Russia engages to stop all military preparations."

Later in the day, at the suggestion of Sir Edward Grey, the Russian Foreign Minister still further modified in the interests of peace the proposition upon which Russia was willing to cease all military preparations.

If Austria consents to stay the march of her armies upon Servian territory, and if, recognizing that the Austro-Servian conflict has assumed the character of a question of European interest, she admits that the great Powers examine the reparation which Servia could accord to the Government of Austria-Hungary without injury to her rights as a sovereign State and to her independence--Russia undertakes to maintain her expectant attitude.

It will be noted that this formula implied that Servia owed some reparation to Austria, and it did not bind Austria to accept the judgment of the Powers as to the character of such reparation.

It simply conceded to the Powers the opportunity to "examine"--not the original controversy between Austria and Servia--but what reparation could be made without a compromise of sovereignty and independence. Austria did not bind itself to do anything except to stay the advance of her army into Servia, while Russia agreed to desist from further preparations or mobilization.

Could the offer have been more liberal? In face of this assurance, how can the Kaiser or Germany reasonably contend that it was the mobilization of the Russian army which precipitated the war.

In the meantime Sir Edward Grey was working tirelessly to suggest some peace formula, upon which the Powers could agree. His suggestions for a conference of the four leading Powers of Europe, other than Russia and Austria, had been negatived by Germany on the frivolous pretext that such a conference was "too formal a method," quite ignoring the fact that its very formality would have necessarily given a "cooling time" to the would-be belligerents. Thereupon Sir Edward Grey urged that,

the German Government should suggest any method by which the influence of the four Powers could be used together to prevent war between Austria and Russia. France agreed. Italy agreed. The whole idea of mediation or mediating influence was ready to be put into operation by any method that Germany could suggest if mine was not acceptable. In fact, mediation was ready to come into operation by any method that Germany thought possible if only Germany would "press the button" in the interests of peace.[70]

[Footnote 70: English White Paper, No. 84.]

Later in the day Sir Edward again repeated his suggestion to the German Ambassador in London and urged that Germany should,

propose some method by which the four Powers should be able to work together to keep the peace of Europe. I pointed out, however, that the Russian Government, while desirous of mediation, regarded it as a condition that the military operations against Servia should be suspended, as otherwise a mediation would only drag on matters and give Austria time to crush Servia. It was of course too late for all military operations against Servia to be suspended. In a short time, I supposed, the Austrian forces would be in Belgrade, and in occupation of some Servian territory. But even then it might be possible to bring some mediation into existence, if Austria, while saying that she must hold the occupied territory until she had complete satisfaction from Servia, stated that she would not advance further, pending an effort of the Powers to mediate between her and Russia.

The only reply that England received to this reiterated request that Germany take the lead in suggesting some acceptable peace formula was set forth in a dispatch from Sir E. Goschen from Berlin to Sir Edward Grey:

I was informed last night that they (the German Foreign Office) had not had time to send an answer yet. To-day, in reply to an inquiry from the French Ambassador as to whether the Imperial Government had proposed any course of action, the [German] Secretary of State said that he felt that time would be saved by communicating with Vienna direct, and that he had asked the Austro-Hungarian Government what would satisfy them. No answer had, however, yet been returned.

The Chancellor told me last night that he was "pressing the button" as hard as he could, and that he was not sure whether he had not gone so far in urging moderation at Vienna that matters had been precipitated rather than otherwise.[71]

[Footnote 71: See English White Paper, No. 84.]

The Court of Public Opinion unfortunately is not favored in the German White Paper with the text of its communication on this subject to Vienna, nor is it given any specifications as to the manner in which the German Chancellor "pressed the button."

What the world knows without documentary proof is that Austria continued its military preparations and operations and that Russia then ordered a general mobilization. The only assurance which Russia received from Austria as a result of the alleged "pressing of the button" is set forth in the following dispatch from the Russian Ambassador at Vienna to Sazonof, dated July 31st:

In spite of the general mobilization I continue to exchange views with Count Berchtold and his collaborators. All insist on the absence of aggressive intentions on the part of Austria against Russia and of ambitions of conquest in regard to Servia, but all equally insist on the necessity for Austria of pursuing to the very end the action begun and of giving to Servia a serious lesson which would constitute a certain guarantee for the future.

This was in effect a flat refusal of all mediatory or otherwise pacific suggestions, for the right of Austria to crush Servia by giving it "a serious lesson"--what such a lesson is let Louvain, Liege, and Rheims witness!--was the crux of the whole question.

Concurrently Sir Edward Goschen telegraphed to Sir Edward Grey that Germany had declared that day the "Kriegsgefahr" and that the German Chancellor had expressed the opinion that "all hope of a peaceful solution of the crisis" was at an end. The British Ambassador then asked the Chancellor,--

whether he could not still put pressure on the authorities at Vienna to do something in the general interests to reassure Russia and to show themselves disposed to continue discussions on a friendly basis. He replied that last night he had begged Austria to reply to your last proposal, and that he had received a reply to the effect that Austrian Minister for Foreign Affairs would take the wishes of the Emperor this morning in the matter.[72]

[Footnote 72: English White Paper, No. 112.]

Here again the world is not favored with the text of the message, in which the Chancellor "begged Austria to reply," nor with that of the Austrian Foreign Minister's reply.

While these events were happening in Berlin and London, the Russian Ambassador in Vienna advised Sazonof "that Austria has determined not to yield to the intervention of the powers and that she is moving troops against Russia as well as Servia."[73]

[Footnote 73: English White Paper, No. 113.]

Russia thereupon, on July 31, ordered a general mobilization of her army.

Concurrently with these interviews, the English Ambassador in Vienna had a conversation with the Austrian Under-Secretary of State and

called his attention to the fact that during the discussion of the Albanian frontier at the London Conference of Ambassadors the Russian Government had stood behind Servia, and that a compromise between the views of Russia and Austria-Hungary resulted with accepted frontier line. Although he[74] spoke in a conciliatory tone, and did not regard the situation as desperate, I could not get from him any suggestion for a similar compromise in the present case. Count Forgach is going this afternoon to see the Russian Ambassador, whom I have informed of the above conversation.[75]

[Footnote 74: The Austrian Under-Secretary of State.]

[Footnote 75: English White Paper, No. 118.]

Notwithstanding all these discouragements and rebuffs, Sir Edward Grey, that unwearying friend of peace, still continued to make a last attempt to preserve peace by instructing the British Ambassador in Berlin to sound the German Foreign Office, as he would sound the Russian Foreign Office,

whether it would be possible for the four disinterested Powers to offer to Austria that they would undertake to see that she obtained full satisfaction of her demands on Servia, provided that they did not impair Servian sovereignty and the integrity of Servian territory. As your Excellency is aware, Austria has already declared her willingness to respect them. Russia might be informed by the four Powers that they would undertake to prevent Austrian demands from going the length of impairing Servian sovereignty and integrity. All Powers would of course suspend further military operations or preparations.

He further instructed Sir Edward Goschen to advise the German Foreign Office that he, Sir Edward Grey, had that morning proposed to the German Ambassador in London,

that if Germany could get any reasonable proposal put forward, which made it clear that Germany and Austria were striving to preserve European peace, and that Russia and France would be unreasonable if they rejected it, I would support it at St. Petersburg and Paris, and go the length of saying that, if Russia and France would not accept it, his Majesty's Government would have nothing more to do with the consequences; that, otherwise, I told the German Ambassador that if France became involved we should be drawn in.[76]

[Footnote 76: English White Paper, No. 111.]

What, then, was the position when the last fatal step was taken? The Czar had pledged his personal honor that no provocative action should be taken by Russia, while peace parleys were in progress, and the Russian Foreign Minister had agreed to cease all military preparations, provided that Austria would recognize that the question of Servia had become one of European interest, and that its sovereignty would be respected.

On July 31st, Austria for the first time in the negotiations agreed to discuss with the Russian Government the merits of the Servian note. Until this eleventh hour Austria had consistently contended that her difficulty with Servia was her own question, in which Russia had no right to intervene, and which it would not under any circumstances even discuss with Russia. For this reason it had refused any time for discussion, abruptly declared war against Servia, commenced its military operations, and repeatedly declined to discuss even the few questions left open in the Servian reply as a basis for further peace parleys.

As recently as July 30th, the Austrian Government had declined or refused any "direct exchange of views with the Russian Government."

But late on July 31st, a so-called "conversation" took place at Vienna between Count Berchtold and the Russian Ambassador, and as a result, the Austrian Ambassador at St. Petersburg was instructed to "converse" with the Russian Minister for Foreign Affairs. This important concession of Austria was conveyed to Sazonof by the Austrian Ambassador at St. Petersburg, who expressed

the readiness of his Government to discuss the substance of the Austrian ultimatum to Servia. M. Sazonof replied by expressing his satisfaction and said it was desirable that the discussions should take place in London with the participation of the Great Powers.

M. Sazonof hoped that the British Government would assume the direction of these discussions. The whole of Europe would be thankful to them. It would be very important that Austria should meanwhile put a stop provisionally to her military action on Servian territory.[77]

[Footnote 77: English White Paper, No. 133.]

It is important to note that Austria's change of heart preceded by some hours the Kaiser's ultimatum to Russia. The former took place some time during the day on July 31st. The latter was sent to St. Petersburg on the midnight of that day. It must also be noted that while Austria thus agreed at the eleventh hour to "discuss the substance of the ultimatum," it did not offer to suspend military preparations or operations and this obviously deprived the concession of its chief value.[78]

[Footnote 78: See Addendum, p. 191-2.]

The cause and purpose of Austria's partial reversal of its policy at present writing can be only a matter of conjecture. When Austria publishes its correspondence with Germany, we may know the truth.

Two theories are equally plausible:

Austria may have taken alarm at the steadfast purpose of Russia to champion the cause of Servia with the sword. If so, its qualified reversal of its bellicose attitude may have induced the war party at Berlin to precipitate the war by the ultimatum to Russia. In that event, Germany's mad policy of war at any cost is even more iniquitous.[79]

[Footnote 79: See Addendum, p. 190, et seq.]

The supposition is equally plausible that Austria had been advised from Berlin that that night Germany would end all efforts to preserve the peace of Europe by an ultimatum to Russia, which would make war inevitable. The case of Germany and Austria at the bar of the world would be made morally stronger if, at the outbreak of hostilities, the attitude of Austria had become more conciliatory. This would make more plausible their contention that the mobilization of Russia and not Austria's flat rejection of all peace overtures had precipitated the conflict.

This much is certain that the Kaiser, with full knowledge that Austria had consented to renew its conferences with Russia, and that a ray of light had broken through the lowering war clouds, either on his own initiative or yielding to the importunities of his military camarilla, directed the issuance of the ultimatum to Russia and thus blasted the last hope of peace.

On midnight of July 31st, the German Chancellor sent the following telegram to the German Ambassador at St. Petersburg:

In spite of still pending mediatory negotiations, and although we ourselves have up to the present moment taken no measures for mobilization, Russia has mobilized her entire army and navy; in other words, mobilized against us also. By these Russian measures we have been obliged, for the safeguarding of the Empire, to announce that danger of war threatens us, which does not yet mean mobilization. Mobilization, however, must follow unless Russia ceases within twelve hours all warlike measures against us and Austria-Hungary and gives us definite assurance thereof. Kindly communicate this at once to M. Sazonof and wire hour of its communication to him.

At midnight the fateful message was delivered. As Sazonof reports the interview:

At midnight the Ambassador of Germany declared to me, by order of his Government, that if within twelve hours, that is at midday of Saturday, we did not commence demobilization, not only in regard to Germany but also in regard to Austria, the German Government would be forced to give the order of mobilization. To my question if this was war the Ambassador replied in the negative, but added that we were very near it.

It will be noted by the italicized portion that Germany did not restrict its demand that Russia cease its preparations against Germany, but it should also desist from any preparations to defend itself or assert its rights against Austria, although Austria had made no offer to suspend either its preparations for war or recall its general mobilization order.

The twelve hours elapsed and Russia, standing upon its dignity as a sovereign nation of equal standing with Germany, declined to answer this unreasonable and most arrogant demand, which under the circumstances was equivalent to a declaration of war.

Simultaneously a like telegram was sent to the Ambassador at Paris, requiring the French Government to state in eighteen hours whether it would remain neutral in the event of a Russian-German war.

The reasons given for this double ultimatum are as disingenuous as the whole course of German diplomacy in this matter. The statement that Germany had pursued any mediatory negotiations was as untrue as its statement that it had taken no measures for mobilization. Equally disingenuous was the statement with respect to the Kriegsgefahr(state of martial law), for when that was declared on July 31st, the railroad, telegraph, and other similar public utilities were immediately taken over by Germany and the movement of troops to the frontier began.

After the fateful ultimatum had thus been given by Germany to Russia, the British Ambassador, pursuant to the instructions of his home office, saw the German Secretary of State on July 31st, and urged him

most earnestly to accept your [Sir Edward Grey's] proposal and make another effort to prevent the terrible catastrophe of a European war.

He [von Jagow] expressed himself very sympathetically toward your proposal, and appreciated your continued efforts to maintain peace but said it was impossible for the Imperial Government to consider any proposal until they had received an answer from Russia to their communication of to-day; this communication, which he admitted had the form of an ultimatum, being that, unless Russia could inform the Imperial Government within twelve hours that she would immediately countermand her mobilization against Germany and Austria, Germany would be obliged on her side to mobilize at once.

I asked his Excellency why they had made their demand even more difficult for Russia to accept by asking them to demobilize in the south as well. He replied that it was in order to prevent Russia from saying that all her mobilization was only directed against Austria.[80]

[Footnote 80: English White Paper, No. 121.]

The German Secretary of State also stated to Sir E. Goschen that both the Emperor William and the German Foreign Office

had even up till last night been urging Austria to show willingness to continue discussions, and telegraphic and telephonic communications from Vienna had been of a promising nature, but Russia's mobilization had spoiled everything.

Here again it must be noted that the telegraphic communications from Vienna have not yet been published by the Austrian Government, nor by the German Foreign Office in its official defense.

Sir Edward Grey's last attempt to preserve peace was on August 1st, when he telegraphed to Sir E. Goschen:

I still believe that it might be possible to secure peace if only a little respite in time can be gained before any great power begins war.

The Russian Government has communicated to me the readiness of Austria to discuss with Russia and the readiness of Austria to accept a basis of mediation which is not open to the objections raised in regard to the formula which Russia originally suggested.

Things ought not to be hopeless so long as Austria and Russia are ready to converse, and I hope that the German Government may be able to make use of the Russian communications referred to above in order to avoid tension. His Majesty's Government are carefully abstaining from any act which may precipitate matters.[81]

[Footnote 81: English White Paper, No. 131.]

At that time the twelve-hour ultimatum to Russia had already expired, but the British Ambassador saw the German Secretary of State on August 1st, and, after submitting to him the substance of Sir Edward Grey's telegram last quoted,

spent a long time arguing with him that the chief dispute was between Austria and Russia, and that Germany was only drawn in as Austria's ally. If, therefore, Austria and Russia were, as was evident, ready to discuss matters and Germany did not desire war on her own account, it seemed to me only logical that Germany should hold her hand and continue to work for a peaceful settlement. Secretary of State for Foreign Affairs said that Austria's readiness to discuss was the result of German influence at Vienna, and, had not Russia mobilized against Germany, all would have been well. But Russia, by abstaining from answering Germany's demand that she should demobilize, had caused Germany to mobilize also. Russia had said that her mobilization did not necessarily imply war, and that she could perfectly well remain mobilized for months without making war. This was not the case with Germany. She had the speed and Russia had the numbers, and the safety of the German Empire forbade that Germany should allow Russia time to bring up masses of troops from all parts of her wide dominions . The situation now was that, though the Imperial Government had allowed her several hours beyond the specified time, Russia had sent no answer. Germany had, therefore, ordered mobilization, and the German representative at St. Petersburg had been instructed within a certain time to inform the Russian Government that the Imperial Government must regard their refusal to answer as creating a state of war.[82]

[Footnote 82: English White Paper, No. 138.]

It will thus be seen that although Germany was urged to the very last to await the result of the conferences, which had just commenced with some slight promise of success between Austria and Russia, it nevertheless elected to declare war against Russia and thus blast beyond possible recall any possibility of peace. Its justification for this course, as stated in the interview with the German Secretary of State last quoted, was that it did not propose to forego its advantage of speed as against the advantage of Russia's numerical superiority. For this there might be some justification, if Russia had shown an unyielding and bellicose attitude, but apart from the fact that Russia had consistently worked in the interests of peace, Germany had the express assurance of the Czar that no provocative action would be taken while peace conferences continued. To disregard these assurances and thus destroy the pacific efforts of other nations, in order not to lose a tactical advantage, was the clearest disloyalty to civilization. In any aspect, Germany could have fully kept its advantage of speed by inducing its ally to suspend its aggressive operations against Servia, for in that event Russia had expressly obligated itself to suspend all military preparations.

As the final document in this shameful chapter of diplomacy, there need only be added the telegram, sent by the German Chancellor to his Ambassador at St. Petersburg on August 1, 1914, in which war was declared by Germany against Russia on the ground that while Germany and Austria should be left free to pursue their aggressive military preparations, Russia should, on the peremptory demand of another nation, cease the mobilization of its armies even for self-defense. It reads:

The Imperial Government has endeavored from the opening of the crisis to lead it to a pacific solution. In accordance with a desire which had been expressed to him by His Majesty the Emperor of Russia, His Majesty the Emperor of Germany in accord with England had applied himself to filling a mediatory role with the Cabinets of Vienna and St. Petersburg, when Russia, without awaiting the result of this, proceeded to the complete mobilization of her forces on land and sea. As a consequence of this threatening measure, motived by no military "presage" on the part of Germany, the German Empire found itself in face of a grave and imminent danger. If the Imperial Government had failed to safeguard herself against this peril it would have compromised the safety and the very existence of Germany. Consequently the German Government saw itself forced to address to the Government of His Majesty the Emperor of all the Russias, an insistence on the cessation of the said military acts. Russia, having refused to accede to (not having thought it should reply to), this demand, and having manifested by this refusal (this attitude) that its action was directed against Germany, I have the honor to make known to your Excellency the following:

His Majesty the Emperor, My August Sovereign, in the name of the Empire, taking up the challenge, considers himself in a state of war with Russia.

The feverish haste with which this fatal step was taken, is shown by the fact that the German Ambassador could not even wait to state whether Russia had refused to answer or answered negatively. This war--thus begun in such mad haste--is likely to be repented of at leisure.

A few hours before this rash and most iniquitous declaration was made the Czar made his last appeal for peace. With equal solemnity and pathos he telegraphed the Kaiser:

I have received your telegram. I comprehend that you are forced to mobilize, but I should like to have from you the same guaranty which I have given you, viz., that these measures do not mean war, and that we shall continue to negotiate for the welfare of our two countries and the universal peace which is so dear to our hearts. With the aid of God it must be possible to our long tried friendship to prevent the shedding of blood. I expect with full confidence your urgent reply.

This touching and magnanimous message does infinite credit to the Czar. Had the Kaiser been as pacific, had he been inspired by the same enlightened spirit in the interests of peace, had he been as truly mindful of the God of nations, whom the Czar thus invoked, it would have been possible to prevent the "shedding of blood," which has now swept away after only three months of war the very flower of the youth of Europe.

To this the Kaiser replied:

I thank You for Your telegram. I have shown yesterday to Your Government the way through which alone war may yet be averted. Although I asked for a reply by to-day noon, no telegram from my Ambassador has reached me with the reply of Your Government. I therefore have been forced to mobilize my army. An immediate, clear and unmistakable reply of Your Government is the sole way to avoid endless misery. Until I receive this reply I am unable, to my great grief, to enter upon the subject of Your telegram. I must ask most earnestly that You, without delay, order Your troops to commit, under no circumstances, the slightest violation of our frontiers.

In this is no spirit of compromise; only the repeated insistence of the unreasonable and in its consequences iniquitous demand that Russia should by demobilizing make itself "naked to its enemies," while Germany and

Austria, without making any real concession in the direction of peace, should be permitted to arm both for offense and defense.

There were practical reasons which made the Kaiser's demand unreasonable. Mobilization is a highly developed and complicated piece of governmental machinery, and even where transportation facilities are of the best, as in Germany and France, the mobilization ordinarily takes about two weeks to complete. In Russia, with limited means of transportation, it was impossible to recall immediately a mobilization order that had gone forward to the remotest corners of the great Empire. The record shows that the Kaiser himself recognized this fact, for in a telegram which he sent on August 1st to King George, with respect to the possible neutralization of England, the Kaiser said:

I just received the communication from Your Government offering French neutrality under the guarantee of Great Britain. Added to this offer was the inquiry whether under these conditions Germany would refrain from attacking France. On technical grounds My mobilization, which had already been proclaimed this afternoon, must proceed against two fronts east and west as prepared; this cannot be countermanded because, I am sorry, Your telegram came so late. But if France offers Me neutrality which must be guaranteed by the British fleet and army, I shall of course refrain from attacking France and employ My troops elsewhere. I hope that France will not become nervous. The troops on My frontier are in the act of being stopped by telegraph and telephone from crossing into France.[83]

[Footnote 83: No such offer had been made. The Kaiser's error was due to a misunderstanding, which had arisen quite honestly between Sir Edward Grey and the German Ambassador in London. King George promptly corrected this misapprehension of the Kaiser.

See also Addendum, p. 192.]

If it were impossible for the Kaiser, with all the exceptional facilities of the German Empire, to arrest his mobilization for "technical" reasons, it was infinitely more difficult for the Czar to arrest immediately his military preparations. The demand of Germany was not that Russia should simply cancel the mobilization order. It was that Russia should "cease within twelve hours all warlike measures," and it demanded a physical impossibility.

In any event, mobilization does not necessarily mean aggression, but simply preparation, as the Czar had so clearly pointed out to the Kaiser in the telegram already quoted. It is the right of a sovereign State and by no code of ethics a casus belli. Germany's demand that Russia should not arm to defend itself, when its prestige as a great European power was at stake and when Austria was pushing her aggressive preparations, treated Russia as an inferior, almost a vassal, State. Its rejection must have been recognized by the Kaiser and his advisers as inevitable, and, on the theory that a man intends the natural consequences of his acts, it must be assumed that the Kaiser in this mad demand at that time desired and intended war, however pacific his purposes may have been when he first took the helm.

Such will be his awful responsibility "to the last syllable of recorded time."

How well prepared Germany was, the sequel developed only too surely. On the following day--August 2d--its troops invaded Luxemburg and an abrupt demand was made upon Belgium for permission to cross its territory.

Upon the declaration of war, the Czar telegraphed to King George of England as follows:

"In this solemn hour, I wish to assure you once more I have done all in my power to avert war."

Such will be the verdict of history.

ADDENDUM

I

THE SUPPRESSED TELEGRAM FROM THE CZAR

It is a curious and suggestive fact that the German Foreign Office in publishing the correspondence between the Kaiser and the Czar omitted one of the most important telegrams.

The Russian Government on January 31, 1915, therefore, made public the following telegram which the Czar sent to the Kaiser on July 29, 1914:

"Thanks for your conciliatory and friendly telegram. Inasmuch as the official message presented to-day by your Ambassador to my Minister was conveyed in a very different tone, I beg you to explain this divergency. It would be right to give over the Austro-Servian problem to The Hague Conference. I trust in your wisdom and friendship."

The German Foreign Office has since explained that they regarded this telegram as too "unimportant" for publication. Comment is unnecessary.

It thus appears that the Czar at the beginning of his correspondence with the Kaiser suggested that the whole dispute be submitted to The Hague Tribunal for adjustment. Servia had already made the same suggestion.

As the world owes the first Hague Convention to the Czar's initiative, it can justly be said to his lasting credit that he at least was loyal to the pacific ideal of that great convention of the nations.

II

THE AUSTRIAN OFFER OF JULY 31, 1914

The author has noted (ante, p. 175) that as the belated offer of Austria on July the 31st "to discuss [with Russia] the substance of the Austrian ultimatum to Servia" did not offer to suspend military preparations or operations, the concession was more nominal than real. The Austrian Red Book converts this inference into a certainty, and makes clear that Austria's pretended change of policy was only diplomatic finesse, as it contained no substantial modification of its uncompromising attitude.

Russia had proposed on July the 30th (ante, p. 166) that "if Austria consents to stay the march of her armies upon Servian territory" and further agreed that the question of "the reparation which Servia could accord to the Government of Austria-Hungary" could be examined by the Great Powers, Russia would suspend her military preparations. As the underlying question was whether Austria should be permitted to subjugate Servia without interference, it was vital that that subjugation should not proceed pending an examination by all interested powers into its justice and ultimate ends.

Sir Edward Grey had previously requested Germany on July the 28th "to use its influence" with the Austrian Government "to the effect that the latter either consider the reply from Belgrade satisfactory or else accept it as a basis for discussion between the Cabinets." The German Foreign Office then instructed the German Ambassador at Vienna "to submit the British proposal to the Vienna Cabinet for its consideration" (Austrian Red Book, No. 43). As a result of this suggestion, Count Berchtold on July the 29th (Austrian Red Book, No. 44) again shut the door upon any compromise by the contention that Austria

"no longer is in a position to meet the Servian reply in the spirit of the British suggestions, since at the time when the German request was presented here, a state of war already existed between the Dual Monarchy and Servia, and thus the Servian reply had been superseded by events."

The only counter-suggestion which Austria then made was as follows:

"Should the British Cabinet be prepared to exert its influence upon the Russian Government for the maintenance of peace among the Great Powers, and for a localization of the war, which had been forced upon us by the Servian agitation of many years' standing, such efforts would meet with the Imperial and Royal Government's appreciation." (Austrian Red Book, No. 44.)

On July 31st the German Ambassador at Vienna, acting on instructions (which instructions are again not disclosed in the German White Book) informed Count Berchtold "of a conversation between Sir Edward Grey and Prince Lichnowsky," in the course of which the British Secretary of State declared to the German Ambassador that Russia felt unable "to treat directly with Austria-Hungary and therefore requested Great Britain to resume her mediation" and that "as a condition of this mediation, however, the Russian Government stipulates the suspension of hostilities in the meanwhile." (Austrian Red Book, No. 51.)

Thereupon Count Berchtold made the eleventh hour offer in question by instructing the Austrian Ambassador at St. Petersburg "to express our readiness to consider Sir Edward Grey's proposition to mediate between us and Servia despite the changes brought about in the situation by Russia's mobilization. Our acceptance, however, is subject to the condition that our military action against Servia shall nevertheless proceed and that the British Cabinet shall induce the Russian Government to stop the mobilization directed against us. It is understood that in this case we would at once cancel our defensive military counter-measures in Galicia, which had been forced upon us by Russia's mobilization." (Austrian Red Book, No. 51.)

This suggestion was fatally objectionable in that it required Russia to suspend its preparations to defend its interests while permitting Austria to proceed with the subjugation of Servia. As the "bone of contention" was this subjugation of Servia, this belated and ostensibly conciliatory proposal of Austria amounted to an absurdity. In that classic of nonsense, Alice in Wonderland, the unreasonable and violent Queen announced in the trial of the Knave the similar procedure of "sentence first, verdict afterwards," and Austria's final proposal was essentially a like folly, for, stripped of diplomatic pretense, it amounted to this, that Austria, while tying Russia's hands, should proceed not merely to sentence but even to execute Servia and subsequently discuss the justice of its action when it had become irremediable.

The possible theory which we suggested (ante, p. 175), that Austria at the eleventh hour may have experienced a change of heart and had adopted a more conciliatory course, is apparently untenable.

III

THE INVASION OF FRANCE ON AUGUST 1ST

It has been Germany's contention that not only did the mobilization of Russia cause the war, but that its eastern and western frontiers were violated by Russian and French soldiers at a time when Germany's intentions were sincerely pacific.

At 7 P.M. on July the 31st, Germany had given France until 1 P.M. of the following day to declare whether it would remain neutral in the event of a Russian-German war, and at that hour Viviani advised the German

Ambassador that France "would do that which her interests dictated." (German White Paper, No. 27.) Notwithstanding France's virtual refusal to meet the demand of Germany, the latter did not declare war on France on that day, and this is the more significant as it immediately declared war on Russia. The German Ambassador remained in Paris until August the 3d, and only then demanded his passports when his position in the French Capitol had become untenable.

In the meantime Germany was awaiting some act of aggression on the part of France, that would enable it under the terms of the Triple Alliance to demand as of right the cooperation of Italy, while France, determined for this and other reasons not to be the aggressor, had withdrawn its troops ten kilometers from the frontier and refused to take any offensive step either before or after the expiration of the ultimatum.

The confidential telegram of the Kaiser to King George suggests the possibility that on August the 1st, about the time that the eighteen-hour ultimatum had expired, Germany was ready and intended to commence an immediate invasion of France, for on that day the Kaiser telegraphs to King George:

"I hope that France will not become nervous. The troops on my frontier are in the act of being stopped by telegraph and telephone from crossing into France." (Ante, p. 187.)

The exact hour when the Kaiser sent the King this message is conjectural. We know from the German White Paper that at 11 A.M. on that day Sir Edward Grey inquired of Prince Lichnowsky over the telephone whether Germany was "in a position to declare that we would not attack France in a war between Germany and Russia in case France should remain neutral."

This message prompted the Kaiser's telegram to King George. How soon thereafter the Kaiser sent his telegram we do not know, but as the impossibility of France's neutrality was recognized in Berlin on receipt of Lichnowsky's telegram by 5 P.M. on that day, it is altogether probable that the Kaiser's telegram was sent between those hours.

If the telegram in question is now analyzed and the fair natural import is given to the Kaiser's language, it would seem that the invasion of France, either before or in any event simultaneously with the expiration of the eighteen-hour ultimatum, had been determined upon by the Kaiser and his military staff, for the Kaiser's intimation that he has "stopped by telegraph and telephone [his army] from crossing into France" fairly implies that previous orders had been given to commence such invasion and that these orders had been hurriedly recalled in the most expeditious way, upon the supposed intimation of Sir Edward Grey that England might guarantee the neutrality of France.

Under these circumstances, with the German Ambassador still at Paris and ostensibly preserving friendly relations, it is evident that the invasion was either to precede or to follow immediately upon the severance of diplomatic relations. This in itself may not be indefensible under international law, but it throws a searchlight upon the contention of Germany that its intentions were pacific and that it had been surprised by a sudden and treacherous attack on the part of Russia, France, and England.

The difficulty, however, is to reconcile this apparent intention of the Kaiser's military staff to invade France on August the 1st and the action of his Foreign Office in failing to make any declaration of war against France and in retaining its Ambassador at Paris and permitting the French Ambassador to remain at Berlin. The diplomatic records abundantly show that this latter policy of the German Foreign Office was followed in the hope that France would become the aggressor, but its inconsistency with the policy of the War Office implied in the Kaiser's telegram is obvious.

Possibly the Kaiser's soldiers and diplomats were not working in complete harmony. It may be true that the many blunders of German diplomats were in part due to the reckless impetuosity of the War Office and it is possible that some of von Bethmann-Hollweg's and von Jagow's diplomatic blunders are more properly attributable to the Kaiser and Moltke.

It is also possible that the natural inference from the Kaiser's language above quoted is misleading and that the telegram to King George did not mean to imply that any orders for an invasion had been cancelled but simply that the army leaders on the Western frontier had been cautioned not to cross the frontier until further orders.

Another possible theory is that the Kaiser for political reasons may have exaggerated the extent of his concession, and magnified the urgency of the situation to induce prompt and favorable action by Great Britain.

But the readiness of Germany to strike a quick and fatal blow at Paris cannot be gainsaid and strangely contrasts with the "injured innocence" protestations that it was treacherously surprised by an unexpected attack. Always with Prussia, "the readiness is all."

IV

THE USE OF THE WORD "ENGLAND"

In making these scattered addenda, I take this occasion to make the amende honorable to some of my readers, who since the first editions of this book appeared have taken exception to my use of the word "England" and "English," where obviously "Great Britain" and "British" were meant. These critics are technically correct, but I hope that they will acquit me of any intention of ignoring any part of the British Empire in using a term, which by common and immemorial usage has been applied throughout the world as synonymous with the great Empire. I should deeply regret it, if any other intention were imputed to me, for in the magnificent struggle which Great Britain has made for the highest ideals of civilization and the basic rights of humanity, no one now or hereafter can ever ignore the heroic part which has been played by Scotland, Ireland, Canada, and the over-sea dominions

May I not plead that the word "England," has to common intent a broader as well as a more restricted meaning and that when the poet, the historian or--as in my case--the student uses the word "England" in reference to a world-wide controversy, no one is likely to misapprehend his meaning. Such use is certainly as common and as generally understood as that of the word "American" as applied to a Citizen of the United States, although in both cases the characterization is not strictly accurate. To my critics in Scotland and Ireland who have made this criticism of my book, I can only say:

"Let my disclaiming from a purposed evil Free me so far in your most generous thoughts, That I have shot mine arrow o'er the house, And hurt my brother."

CHAPTER IX

THE CASE OF BELGIUM

The callous disregard by Germany of the rights of Belgium is one of the most shocking exhibitions of political iniquity in the history of the world.

That it has had its parallel in other and less civilized ages may be freely admitted, but until German scientists, philosophers, educators, and even doctors of divinity attempted to justify this wanton outrage, it had been hoped that mankind had made some progress since the times of Wallenstein and Tilly.

The verdict of Civilization in this respect will be little affected by the ultimate result of the war, for even if Germany should emerge from this titanic conflict as victor, and become, as it would then undoubtedly become, the first power in the world, it would none the less be a figure for the "time of scorn to point his slow unmoving finger at." To the eulogists of Alexander the Great, Seneca was wont to say, "Yes, but he murdered Callisthenes," and to the eulogists of victorious Germany, if indeed it shall prove victorious, the wise and just of all future ages will say, "Yes, but it devastated Belgium."

The fact that many distinguished and undoubtedly sincere partisans of Germany have attempted to justify this atrocious rape, suggests a problem of psychology rather than of logic or ethics. It strongly illustrates a too familiar phenomenon that great intellectual and moral astigmatism is generally incident to any passionate crisis in human history. It shows how pitifully unstable the human intellect is when a great man like Dr. Haeckel, a scholar and historian like Dr. von Mach, or a doctor of divinity like Dr. Dryander, can be so warped with the passions of the hour as to ignore the clearest considerations of political morality.

At the outbreak of the present war Belgium had taken no part whatever in the controversy and was apparently on friendly relations with all the Powers. It had no interest whatever in the Servian question. A thrifty, prosperous people, inhabiting the most densely populated country of Europe, and resting secure in the solemn promises, not merely of Germany, but of the leading European nations that its neutrality should be respected, it calmly pursued the even tenor of its way, and was as unmindful of the disaster, which was so suddenly to befall it, as the people of Pompeii were on the morning of the great eruption when they thronged the theatre in the pursuit of pleasure and disregarded the ominous curling of the smoke from the crater of Vesuvius.

On April 19, 1839, Belgium and Holland signed a treaty which provided that "Belgium forms an independent state of perpetual neutrality." To insure that neutrality, Prussia, France, Great Britain, Austria, and Russia on the same date signed a treaty, by which it was provided that these nations jointly "became the guarantors" of such "perpetual neutrality."

In his recent article on the war, George Bernard Shaw, who is inimitable as a farceur but not quite convincing as a jurist, says:

As all treaties are valid only rebus sic stantibus, and the state of things which existed at the date of the Treaty of London (1839) had changed so much since then ... that in 1870 Gladstone could not depend on it, and resorted to a special temporary treaty not now in force, the technical validity of the 1839 treaty is extremely doubtful.

Unfortunately for this contention, the Treaty of 1870, to which Mr. Shaw refers, provided for its own expiration after twelve months and then added:

And on the expiration of that time the independence and neutrality of Belgium will, so far as the high contracting parties are respectively concerned, continue to rest as heretofore on the 1st Article of the Quintuple Treaty of the 19th of April, 1839.

Much has been made by Mr. Shaw and others of an excerpt from a speech of Mr. Gladstone in 1870. In that speech, Mr. Gladstone, as an abstract proposition, declined to accept the broad statement that under all circumstances the obligations of a treaty might continue, but there is nothing to justify the belief that Mr. Gladstone in any respect questioned either the value or the validity of the Treaty of 1839 with respect to Belgium.

Those who invoke the authority of Gladstone should remember that he also said:

We have an interest in the independence of Belgium which is wider than that which we may have in the literal operation of the guarantee. It is found in the answer to the question whether, under the circumstances of the case, this country, endowed as it is with influence and power, would quietly stand by and witness the perpetration of the direst crime that ever stained the pages of history, and thus become participators in the sin.

These words of the great statesman read as a prophecy.

While these treaties were simply declaratory of the rights, which Belgium independently enjoyed as a sovereign nation, yet this solemn guarantee of the great Powers of Europe was so effective that even in 1870, when France and Germany were locked in vital conflict, and the question arose whether Prussia would disregard her treaty obligation, the Iron Chancellor, who ordinarily did not permit moral considerations to warp his political policies, wrote to the Belgian minister in Berlin on July 22, 1870:

In confirmation of my verbal assurance, I have the honor to give in writing a declaration, which, in view of the treaties in force, is quite superfluous, that the Confederation of the North and its allies (Germany) will respect the neutrality of Belgium on the understanding of course that it is respected by the other belligerent.

At that time, Belgium had so fine a sense of honor, that although it was not inconsistent with the principles of international law, yet in order to discharge her obligations of neutrality in the spirit as well as the letter, she restricted the clear legal right of her people to supply arms and ammunition to the combatants, thus construing the treaty to her own disadvantage.

It can be added to the credit of both France and Prussia that in their great struggle of 1870-71, each scrupulously respected that neutrality, and France carried out her obligations to such an extreme that although Napoleon and his army could have at one time escaped from Sedan into Belgium, and renewed the attack and possibly--although not probably--saved France, if they had seen fit to violate that neutrality, rather than break the word of France the Emperor Napoleon and his army consented to the crowning humiliation of Sedan.

In the year 1911, in the course of a discussion in Belgium in respect to the fortifications at Flushing, certain Dutch newspapers asserted that in the event of a Franco-German war, the neutrality of Belgium would be violated by Germany. It was then suggested that if a declaration were made to the contrary in the Reichstag, that such a declaration, "would be calculated to appease public opinion and to calm its suspicions."

This situation was communicated to the present German Chancellor, von Bethmann-Hollweg, who instructed the German Ambassador at Brussels to assure the Belgian Foreign Minister,

that he was most appreciative of the sentiment which had inspired our [Belgium's] action. He declared that Germany had no intention of violating our neutrality, but he considered that by making a declaration publicly, Germany would weaken her military preparation with respect to France, and being reassured in the northern quarter would direct her forces to the eastern quarter.[84]

[Footnote 84: Belgian Gray Book, enclosure No. 12.]

Germany's recognition of the continuing obligation of this treaty was also shown when the question of Belgium's neutrality was suggested at a debate in the Reichstag on April 29, 1913. In the course of that debate a member of the Social Democratic Party said:

In Belgium the approach of a Franco-German war is viewed with apprehension, because it is feared that Germany will not respect Belgian neutrality.[85]

[Footnote 85: Idem.]

Herr von Jagow, Secretary of State for Foreign Affairs, replied: "The neutrality of Belgium is determined by international conventions, and Germany is resolved to respect these conventions."

This declaration did not satisfy another member of the Social Democratic

Party. Herr von Jagow observed that he had nothing to add to the clear statement which he had uttered with reference to the relations between Germany and Belgium.

In reply to further interrogations from a member of the Social Democratic Party, Herr von Heeringen, Minister of War, stated: "Belgium does not play any part in the justification of the German scheme of military reorganization; the scheme is justified by the position of matters in the East. Germany will not lose sight of the fact that Belgian neutrality is guaranteed by international treaties."

A member of the same party, having again referred to Belgium, Herr von Jagow again pointed out that his declaration regarding Belgium was sufficiently clear.[86]

[Footnote 86: Belgian Gray Book, No. 12.]

On July 31, 1914, the Belgian Foreign Minister, in a conversation with Herr von Below, the German Minister at Brussels, asked him whether he knew of the assurance which, as above stated, had been given by von Bethmann-Hollweg through the German Ambassador at Brussels to the Government at Belgium in 1911, and Herr von Below replied that he did, and added, "that he was certain that the sentiments to which expression was given at that time had not changed."

Thus on July 31, 1914, Germany, through its accredited representative at Brussels, repeated the assurances contained in the treaty of 1839, as reaffirmed in 1870, and again reaffirmed in 1911 and 1913.

Germany's moral obligation had an additional express confirmation.

The second International Peace Conference was held at The Hague in 1907. There were present the representatives of forty-four nations, thus making as near an approach to the poet's dream of the "federation of the world" and the "parliament of man" as has yet been possible in the slow progress of mankind.

That convention agreed upon a certain declaration of principles, and among the signatures appended to the document was the representative of His Majesty, the German Emperor.

They agreed upon certain principles of international morality, most of them simply declaratory of the uncodified international law then existing, and these were subsequently ratified by formal treaties of the respective governments, including Germany, which were deposited in the archives of The Hague. While this treaty as an express covenantwas not binding, unless all belligerents signed it, yet, it recognized an existing moral obligation. The Hague Peace Conference proceeded to define the rights of neutral powers, and in so doing simply reaffirmed the existing international law.

The pertinent parts of this great compact, with reference to the sanctity of neutral territory, are as follows:

CONVENTION V

CHAPTER I.--"THE RIGHTS AND DUTIES OF NEUTRAL POWERS"

ARTICLE I.

The territory of neutral Powers is inviolable.

ARTICLE II.

Belligerents are forbidden to move troops or convoys of either munitions of war or supplies across the territory of a neutral Power.

ARTICLE X.

The fact of a neutral Power resisting, even by force, attempts to violate its neutrality cannot be regarded as a hostile act.

Notwithstanding these assurances, it had been from time to time intimated by German military writers, and notably by Bernhardi, that Germany would, in the event of a future war, make a quick and possibly a fatal blow at the heart of France by invading Belgium upon the first declaration of hostilities, and it was probably these intimations that led the Belgian Government on

July 24, 1914, to consider:

Whether in the existing circumstances, it would not be proper to address to the Powers, who had guaranteed Belgium's independence and its neutrality, a communication for the purpose of confirming to them its resolution to carry out the international duties which are imposed upon it by treaties in the event of war breaking out on the Belgian frontiers.

Confiding in the good faith of France and Germany, the Belgian Government concluded that any such declaration was premature.

On August 2, 1914, the war having already broken out, the Belgian Foreign Minister took occasion to tell the German Ambassador that France had reaffirmed its intention to respect the neutrality of Belgium, and Herr von Below, the German Ambassador, after thanking Davignon for his information, added that up to the present he had not been

instructed to make us any official communication, but we were aware of his personal opinion respecting the security with which we had the right to regard our eastern neighbors. I [Davignon] replied at once that all we knew of the intentions of the latter, intentions set forth in many former interviews, did not allow us to doubt their [Germany's] perfectly correct attitude toward Belgium.

It thus appears that as late as August 2, 1914, Germany had not given to Belgium any intimation as to its intention, and, what is more important, it had not either on that day or previously made any charge that Belgium had in any way violated its obligations of neutrality, or that France had committed any overt act in violation thereof.

On July 31, 1914, England, not unreasonably apprehensive as to the sincerity of Germany's oft-repeated protestations of good faith, directed the English Ambassadors at Paris and Berlin to ask the respective governments of those countries "whether each is prepared to respect the neutrality of Belgium, provided it is violated by no other Power."

This question was communicated by Sir Edward Grey to the Belgian Government, with the addition that he (Sir Edward Grey) asked that "the

Belgian Government will maintain to the utmost of her power her neutrality which I desire, and expect other Powers to uphold and observe."

Pursuant to these instructions, the English Ambassador to Paris, on the night of July 31, 1914, called upon Viviani, the Minister of Foreign Affairs, and on the same night received a reply which is reported by Sir F. Bertie to Sir Edward Grey, as follows:

French Government is resolved to respect the neutrality of Belgium, and it would be only in the event of some other Power violating that neutrality that France might find herself under the necessity, in order to assure defense of her own security, to act otherwise. This assurance has been given several times. The President of the Republic spoke of it to the King of the Belgians, and the French Minister to Brussels has spontaneously renewed the assurance to the Belgian Minister for Foreign Affairs to-day.[87]

[Footnote 87: English White Paper, No. 125.]

Confirming this, the French Minister at Brussels, on August 1st, made to the Belgian Foreign Minister the following declaration:

I am authorized to declare that in the event of an international conflict, the government of the Republic will, as it has always declared, respect the neutrality of Belgium. In the event of this neutrality not being respected by another Power, the French Government, in order to insure its own defense, might be led to modify its attitude.[88]

[Footnote 88: Belgian Gray Paper, No. 15.]

On July 31, 1914, the English Ambassador at Berlin saw the German Secretary of State, and submitted Sir Edward Grey's pointed interrogation, and the only reply that was given was that "he must consult the Emperor and the Chancellor before he could possibly answer," and the German Secretary of State very significantly added that for strategic reasons it was "very doubtful whether they would return any answer at all."

Goschen also submitted the matter to the German Chancellor, who also evaded the question by stating that "Germany would in any case desire to know the reply returned to you [the English Ambassador] by the French Government."

That these were mere evasions the events on the following day demonstrated.

On August 1st, Sir Edward Grey saw the German Ambassador in London, and the following significant conversation took place:

I told the German Ambassador to-day that the reply of the German Government with regard to the neutrality of Belgium was a matter of very great regret, because the neutrality of Belgium affected feeling in this country. If Germany could see her way to give the same assurance as that which had been given by France it would materially contribute to relieve anxiety and tension here. On the other hand, if there were a violation of the neutrality of Belgium by one combatant, while the other respected it, it would be extremely difficult to restrain public feeling in this country. I said that we had been discussing this question at a Cabinet meeting, and as I was authorized to tell him this I gave him a memorandum of it.

He asked me whether, if Germany gave a promise not to violate Belgian neutrality, we would engage to remain neutral.

I replied that I could not say that; our hands were still free, and we were considering what our attitude should be. All I could say was that our attitude would be determined largely by public opinion here, and that the neutrality of Belgium would appeal very strongly to public opinion here. I did not think that we could give a promise of neutrality on that condition alone.[89]

[Footnote 89: English White Paper, No. 123.]

On the following day, August 2d, the German Minister at Brussels handed to the Belgian Foreign Office the following "highly confidential" document. After stating that "the German Government has received reliable information, according to which the French forces intend to march on the Meuse, by way of Givet and Namur," and after suggesting a "fear that Belgium, in spite of its best will, will be in no position to repulse such a largely developed French march without aid," the document adds:

It is an imperative duty for the preservation of Germany to forestall this attack of the enemy. The German Government would feel keen regret if Belgium should regard as an act of hostility against herself the fact that the measures of the enemies of Germany oblige her on her part to violate Belgian territory.[90]

[Footnote 90: Belgian Gray Book, No. 20.]

Some hours later, at 1.30 A.M. on August 3d, the German Minister aroused the Belgian Secretary General for the Minister of Foreign Affairs from his slumbers and,

asked to see Baron von der Elst. He told him that he was instructed by his Government to inform us that French dirigibles had thrown bombs, and that a patrol of French cavalry, violating international law, seeing that war was not declared, had crossed the frontier.

The Secretary General asked Herr von Below where these events had taken place; in Germany, he was answered. Baron von der Elst observed that in that case he could not understand the object of his communication. Herr von Below said that these acts, contrary to international law, were of a nature to make one expect that other acts contrary to international law would be perpetrated by France.[91]

[Footnote 91: Belgian Gray Paper, No. 21.]

As to these last communications, it should be noted that the German Government, neither then nor at any subsequent time, ever disclosed to the world the "reliable information," which it claimed to have of the intentions of the French Government, and the event shows beyond a possibility of contradiction that at that time France was unprepared to make any invasion of Belgium or even to defend its own north-eastern frontier.

It should further be noted that the alleged aggressive acts of France, which were made the excuse for the invasion of Belgium, according to the statement of the German Ambassador himself, did not take place in Belgium but in Germany.

On August 3d, at 7 o'clock in the morning, Belgium served upon the German Ambassador at Brussels the following reply to the German ultimatum, which, after quoting the substance of the German demand, continued:

This note caused profound and painful surprise to the King's Government.

The intentions which it attributed to France are in contradiction with the express declarations which were made to us on the 1st August in the name of the Government of the Republic.

Moreover, if, contrary to our expectation, a violation of Belgian neutrality were to be committed by France, Belgium would fulfill all her international duties, and her army would offer the most vigorous opposition to the invader.

The treaties of 1839, confirmed by the treaties of 1870, establish the independence and the neutrality of Belgium under the guarantee of the Powers, and particularly of the Government of His Majesty the King of Prussia.

Belgium has always been faithful to her international obligations; she has fulfilled her duties in a spirit of loyal impartiality; she has neglected no effort to maintain her neutrality or to make it respected.

The attempt against her independence, with which the German Government threatens her, would constitute a flagrant violation of international law. No strategic interest justifies the violation of that law.

The Belgian Government would, by accepting the propositions which are notified to her, sacrifice the honor of the nation while at the same time betraying her duties toward Europe.

Conscious of the part Belgium has played for more than eighty years in the civilization of the world, she refuses to believe that her independence can be preserved only at the expense of the violation of her neutrality.

If this hope were disappointed the Belgian Government has firmly resolved to repulse by every means in her power any attack upon her rights.

In the records of diplomacy there are few nobler documents than this. Belgium then knew that she was facing possible annihilation. Every material interest suggested acquiescence in the peremptory demands of her powerful neighbor. In the belief that then so generally prevailed, but which recent events have somewhat modified, the success of Germany seemed probable, and if so, Belgium, by facilitating the triumph of Germany, would be in a position to participate in the spoils of the victory.

If Belgium had regarded her honor as lightly as Germany and felt that the matter of self-preservation would excuse any moral dereliction, she would have imitated the example of Luxemburg, also invaded, and permitted free passage to the German army without essential loss of her material prosperity, but with a fatal sacrifice to her national honor.

Even under these conditions Belgium evidently entertained a hope that Germany at the last moment would not, in view of its promises and the protest of Belgium, commit this foul outrage.

The military attach?of the French Government, being apprised of Germany's virtual declaration of war, offered "the support of five French army corps to the Belgian Government," and in reply Belgium, still jealously regardful of her obligation of neutrality, replied:

We are sincerely grateful to the French Government for offering eventual support. In the actual circumstances, however, we do not propose to appeal to the guarantee of the Powers. The Belgian Government will decide later on the action which they think it necessary to take.

As in Caesar's time, the Belg? of all the tribes of Gaul, are in truth "the bravest."

Later in the evening, the King of Belgium met his Ministers, and the offer of France was communicated to them, and again the Belgian Government, still reposing some confidence in the Punic faith of Prussia, decided not to appeal to the guaranteeing Powers, or to avail itself of the offers of France.

On the following morning at 6 o'clock the German Minister handed this formal declaration of war to the Belgian Government:

I have been instructed, and have the honor to inform your Excellency, that in consequence of the Government of His Majesty the King having declined the well-intentioned proposals submitted to them by the Imperial Government, the latter will, deeply to their regret, be compelled to carry out--if necessary by force of arms--the measures of security which have been set forth as indispensable in view of the French menaces.

Here again, no active violation of Belgium's neutrality by France is alleged, only "French menaces."

The conjecture is plausible that in the case of the Prussian General Staff, it was their "own hard dealings" which thus taught them to "suspect the thoughts of others."

On that day the German troops crossed the Belgian frontier and hostilities began.

On the same day, at the great session of the Reichstag, when the Imperial Chancellor attempted to justify to the world the hostile acts of Germany, and especially the invasion of Belgium, the pretended defense was thus bluntly stated by the German Premier:

We are now in a state of necessity and necessity knows no law. Our troops have occupied Luxemburg and perhaps are already on Belgian soil. Gentlemen, that is contrary to the dictates of international law. It is true that the French Government has declared at Brussels that France is willing to respect the neutrality of Belgium, so long as her opponent respects it. We knew, however, that France stood ready for invasion. France could wait, but we could not wait. A French movement upon our flank upon the lower Rhine might have been disastrous. So we were compelled to override the just protest of the Luxemburg and Belgian Governments. The wrong--I speak openly--that we are committing we will endeavor to make good as soon as our military goal has been reached. Anybody who is threatened, as we are threatened, and is fighting for his highest possessions, can only have one thought--how he is to hack his way through.

It will be noted that on this occasion, when above all other occasions it was not only the duty, but to the highest interests of Germany, to give to the world any substantial reason for violating the neutrality of Belgium, the defense of Germany is rested upon the ground of self-interest,--euphemistically called "necessity,"--and upon none other.

While von Bethmann-Hollweg's statement does state that "France held herself in readiness to invade Belgium," there was no intimation that France had done so, or had any immediate intention of doing so. On the contrary, it was added, "France could wait, we (Germany) could not." If Belgium had forfeited its rights by undue favors to France or England, why did the Chancellor characterize its protest as "just"?

How Germany fulfilled the promise of its Chancellor, to "make good" the admitted wrong which it did Belgium, subsequent events have shown.

It may be questioned whether, since the Thirty Years' War, any country has been subjected to such general devastating horrors. So little effort has been taken by the conqueror to lessen the inevitable suffering, that fines have been levied upon this impoverished people, which would be oppressive even in a period of prosperity. It is announced from Holland, as this book goes to press, that Germany has imposed upon this war-desolated country a fine of $7,000,000 per month and an especial fine of $75,000,000, for its "violation of neutrality."

Were this episode not a tragedy, the sardonic humor, which caused the German General Staff to impose this monstrous fine upon Belgium for its "violation of neutrality," would have the tragi-comical aspects of Bedlam. It recalls the fable of the wolf who complained that the lamb was muddying the stream and when the lamb politely called the wolf's attention to the fact that it stood lower down on the river side than the wolf, the latter announced its intention to devour the lamb in any event. Such is probably the intention of Prussia. If it prevail Belgium as an independent State will cease to exist and it will be mourned as Poland is. Like Poland, it may have a resurrection.

The war having thus commenced between Germany and Belgium, the brave ruler of the latter country--"every inch a King"--addressed to the King of England the following appeal:

Remembering the numerous proofs of your Majesty's friendship and that of your predecessor, and the friendly attitude of England in 1870 and the proof of friendship you have just given us again, I make a supreme appeal to the diplomatic intervention of your Majesty's Government to safeguard the integrity of Belgium.[92]

[Footnote 92: Belgian Gray Paper, No. 25.]

In reply to that appeal, which no chivalrous nation could have disregarded, Sir Edward Grey immediately, on August 4th, advised the British Ambassador in Berlin as follows:

We hear that Germany has addressed a note to Belgian Minister for Foreign Affairs stating that German Government will be compelled to carry out, if necessary by force of arms, the measures considered indispensable.

We are also informed that Belgian territory has been violated at Gemmenich.

In these circumstances, and in view of the fact that Germany declined to give the same assurance respecting Belgium as France gave last week in reply to our request made simultaneously at Berlin and Paris, we must repeat that request, and ask that a satisfactory reply to it and to my telegram of this morning be received here by 12 o'clock to-night. If not, you are instructed to ask for your passports, and to say that his Majesty's Government feel bound to take all steps in their power to uphold the neutrality of Belgium and the observance of a treaty to which Germany is as much a party as ourselves.[93]

[Footnote 93: English White Paper. No. 159.]

Thereupon Sir Edward Goschen, the British Ambassador in Berlin, called upon the Secretary of State and stated in the name of His Majesty's Government that unless the Imperial Government

could give the assurance by 12 o'clock that night that they would proceed no further with their violation of the Belgian frontier and stop their advance, I had been instructed to demand my passports and inform the Imperial Government that His Majesty's Government would have to take all steps in their power to uphold the neutrality of Belgium and the observance of a treaty to which Germany was as much a party as themselves.

Herr von Jagow replied that to his great regret he could give no other answer than that which he had given me earlier in the day, namely, that the safety of the Empire rendered it absolutely necessary that the Imperial troops should advance through Belgium. I gave his Excellency a written summary of your telegram and, pointing out that you had mentioned 12 o'clock as the time when His Majesty's Government would expect an answer, asked him whether, in view of the terrible consequences which would necessarily ensue, it were not possible even at the last moment that their answer should be reconsidered. He replied that if the time given were even twenty-four hours or more, his answer must be the same. I said that in that case I should have to demand my passports. This interview took place at about 7 o'clock....

I then said that I should like to go and see the Chancellor, as it might be, perhaps, the last time I should have an opportunity of seeing him. He begged me to do so. I found the Chancellor very agitated. His Excellency at once began a harangue, which lasted for about twenty minutes. He said that the step taken by His Majesty's Government was terrible to a degree; just for a word--"neutrality," a word which in war time had so often been disregarded-- just for a scrap of paper Great Britain was going to make war on a kindred nation who desired nothing better than to be friends with her. All his efforts in that direction had been rendered useless by this last terrible step, and the policy to which, as I knew, he had devoted himself since his accession to office had tumbled down like a house of cards. What we had done was unthinkable; it was like striking a man from behind while he was fighting for his life against two assailants. He held Great Britain responsible for all the terrible events that might happen. I protested strongly against that statement, and said that, in the same way as he and Herr von Jagow wished me to understand that for strategical reasons it was a matter of life and death to Germany to advance through Belgium and violate the latter's neutrality, so I would wish him to understand that it was, so to speak, a matter of "life and death" for the honor of Great Britain that she should keep her solemn engagement to do her utmost to defend Belgium's neutrality if attacked. That solemn compact simply had to be kept, or what confidence could any one have in engagements given by Great Britain in the future? The Chancellor said, "But at what price will that compact have been kept. Has the British Government thought of that?" I hinted to his Excellency as plainly as I could that fear of consequences could hardly be regarded as an excuse for breaking solemn engagements, but his Excellency was so excited, so evidently overcome by the news of our action, and so little disposed to hear reason, that I refrained from adding fuel to the flame by further argument....[94]

[Footnote 94: British White Paper, No. 160.]

Here again it is most significant, in view of the subsequent clumsily framed defense by German apologists, to note that the German Secretary of State, Herr von Jagow, and his superior, the German Chancellor, did not pretend to suggest that the invasion of Belgium was due to any overt act of France.

With even greater frankness von Jagow stated the real purpose, which was, "to advance into France by the quickest and easiest way," and to "avoid the more Southern route," which, "in view of the paucity of roads and the strength of the fortresses," would have entailed "great loss of time."

The damning conclusion as to the guilt of Germany, which irresistibly follows from these admitted facts, is sought to be overborne by a pamphlet entitled "The Truth about Germany," and subscribed to by a number of distinguished Germans, who are in turn vouched for in America by Professor John W. Burgess of Columbia College. He tells us that they are the "salt of the earth," and "among the greatest thinkers, moralists, and philanthropists of the age." To overbear the doubter with the weight of such authority we are told that this defense has the support of the great theologian, Harnack, the sound and accomplished political scientist and economist, von Schmoller, the distinguished philologian, von Wilamowitz, the well-known historian, Lamprecht, the profound statesman, von Posadowsky, the brilliant diplomatist, von Below, the great financier, von Gwinner, the great promoter of trade and commerce, Ballin, the great inventor, Siemens, the brilliant preacher of the Gospel, Dryander, and the indispensable Director in the Ministry of Education, Schmidt. (The adjectives are those of Professor Burgess.)

The average American, as indeed the average citizen of any country, when his natural passions are not unduly aroused, is apt to take a very prosaic and dispassionate view of such matters, and when he has reached his conclusion based upon everyday, commonplace morality, he is not apt to be shaken even by an imposing array of names, fortified by an enthusiastic excess of grandiloquent adjectives. The aristocracy of brains has no monopoly of truth, which is often best grasped by the democracy of common sense.

The defense of these notable representatives of German thought seems to be based upon the wholly unsupported assertion that "England and France were resolved not to respect the neutrality of Belgium."

They say:

It would have been a crime against the German people if the German General Staff had not anticipated this intention. The inalienable right of self-defense gives the individual, whose very existence is at stake, the moral liberty to resort to weapons which would be forbidden except in times of peril. As Belgium would, nevertheless, not acquiesce in a friendly neutrality, which would permit the unobstructed passage of German troops through small portions of her territory, although her integrity was guaranteed, the German General Staff was obliged to force the passage in order to avoid the necessity of meeting the enemy on the most unfavorable ground.

In other words, it seemed preferable to the German General Staff that it should fight in France rather than in Germany, and for this reason Belgium must be ruined.

Notwithstanding this and similar propositions, which are so abhorrent in their political immorality, it is yet gravely suggested by Dr. Dernberg and others that Bernhardi's philosophy does not reflect the true thought of the Prussian ruling classes. Here are representative theologians, economists, historians, statesmen, diplomatists, financiers, inventors, and educators, who, in invoking the support of the educated classes in the United States, deliberately subscribe to a proposition at which even Machiavelli might have gagged.

We are further told that "the German troops, with their iron discipline will respect the personal property and liberty of the individual in Belgium just as they did in France in 1870," and these scientists, philosophers, and doctors of divinity add that "Belgium would have been wise, if it had permitted the passage of the German troops," for the Belgian people "would have fared well from the business point of view, for the army would have proved a good customer and paid well."

To this defense we are led in the last analysis, that Belgium should have preferred cash to her honor, just as the German General Staff preferred dishonor to the sacrifice of an immediate military advantage.

The possibilities of moral casuistry have been severely tested in the attempt of these apologists for Germany to defend the forcible invasion of Belgium.

The ethical question has been made quite unnecessarily to pivot upon the express contractual obligations of England, Germany, and France with respect to the neutrality of Belgium. The indictment of Germany has been placed upon the sound but too narrow ground that by the Treaty of 1839, and The Hague Convention of 1907, Germany had obligated itself by a solemn pledge to respect the neutrality both of Luxemburg and Belgium.

If, however, there had been no Hague Convention and no Treaty of 1839, and if Germany, England, and France had never entered into reciprocal obligations in the event of war to respect Belgium's neutrality, nevertheless upon the broadest considerations of international law the invasion without its consent would be without any justification whatever.

It is a fundamental axiom of international law that each nation is the sole and exclusive judge of the conditions under which it will permit an alien to cross its frontiers. Its territory is sacrosanct. No nation may invade the territory of another without its consent. To do so by compulsion is an act of war. Each nation's land is its castle of asylum and defense. This fundamental right of Belgium should not be confused or obscured by balancing the subordinate equities between France, Germany, and England with respect to their formal treaty obligations.

Belgium's case has thus been weakened in the forum of public opinion by too insistent reference to the special treaties. The right of Belgium and of its citizens as individuals, to be secure in their possessions rests upon the sure foundation of inalienable right and is guarded by the immutable principle of moral law, "Thou shalt not steal." It was well said by Alexander Hamilton:

The sacred rights of man are not to be searched for in old parchments and musty records; they are written as with a sunbeam in the whole volume of human nature by the hand of Divinity itself and can never be erased by mortal power.

This truth can be illustrated by an imaginary instance. Let us suppose that the armies of the Kaiser had made the progress which they so confidently anticipated, and had not simply captured Paris, but had also invaded England, and that, in an attempt to crush the British Empire, the German General Staff planned an invasion of Canada. Let us further suppose that Germany thereupon served upon the United States such an arrogant demand as it made upon Belgium, requiring the United States to permit it to land an army in New York, with the accompanying assurance that neither its territory nor independence would be injured, and that Germany would generously reimburse it for any damage.

Let us further suppose--and it is not a very fanciful supposition--that the United States would reply to the German demand that under no circumstances should a German force be landed in New York or its territory be used as a base of hostile operations against Canada. To carry out the analogy in all its details, let us then suppose that the German fleet should land an army in the city of New York, arrest its Mayor, and check the first attempt of its outraged inhabitants to defend the city by demolishing the Cathedral, the Metropolitan Art Gallery, the City Hall and other structures, and shooting down remorselessly large numbers of citizens, because a few non-combatants had not accepted the invasion with due humility.

Although Germany had not entered into any treaty to respect the territory of the United States, no one would seriously contend that Germany would be justified in such an invasion.

The alleged invalidation of the treaty of 1839 being thus unimportant, Dr. Dernberg and Professor von Mach fall back upon the only remaining defense, that France had already violated the neutrality of Belgium with the latter's consent. Of this there is no evidence whatever. We have, on the contrary, the express assurance, which France gave on the eve of the German invasion both to Belgium and England, that it would not violate the rights of Belgium, and in addition we have the significant fact that when Belgium was invaded, and it was vitally necessary that the French Army should go with all possible speed to its relief and thus stop the invasion and save France itself from invasion, it was ten days before France could send any adequate support. Unhappily it was then too late.

If it were true that France intended to invade Belgium, then of all the blunders that the German Foreign Office has made, the greatest was that it did not permit France to carry out this step, for it would have palliated the action of Germany in meeting such violation by a similar invasion, and it would thus have been an immeasurable gain for Germany and a greater injury to France.

Germany's greatest weakness to-day is its moral isolation. It stands condemned by the judgment of the civilized world. No physical power it can exercise can compensate for this loss of moral power. Even success will be too dearly bought at such a price. There are things which succeed better than success. Truth is one of them.

Under the plea of necessity, which means Germany's desire to minimize its losses of life, Germany has turned Belgium into a shambles, trampled a peaceful nation under foot and almost crushed its soul beneath the iron tread of its mighty armies.

Almost wounded unto death, and for a time prostrate under the heel of the conqueror, the honor of Belgium shines unsullied by any selfish interests, personal dishonor, or lack of courage.

It is claimed that there were officers of the French Army in Liege and Namur before the war broke out. Neither names nor dates have been given, and the allegation might be fairly dismissed because of the very vagueness of the charge. But even if it were true, international law does not forbid the officers of one nation serving with the armies of another. German officers have for many years been thus employed in Turkey and engaged in training and developing the Turkish Army, but no one has ever contended that the employment by that country of German military officers was a violation of neutrality, or gave rise to a casus belli.

It is wholly probable that there were some German officers in Belgium before the war commenced, and if not, there were certainly hundreds of spies, of whose pernicious activities the Belgian people were to learn later to their infinite sorrow, but because Germany employed an elaborate system of espionage in Belgium, it could not justify France in invading its territory without its permission.

To a lawyer, who has had experience in the judicial ascertainment of truth, there is one consideration that justifies him in disposing of all these vague allegations with respect to French activities in Belgium on the eve of the war, and that is that Germany has not only failed to give any testimony in support of the charges, but it never suggested this defense until the judgment of the civilized world had branded it with an ineffaceable stain.

Professor von Mach, a former educator of Harvard University and an apologist for Germany, feels this poverty of evidence and has rather naively suggested an adjournment of the case. He says:

Did French officers remain in Liege or in any other Belgian fortress after hostilities had begun, and did France plan to go through Belgium? Germany has officially made both claims. The first can easily be substantiated by The Supreme Court of Civilization by an investigation of the prisoners of war taken in Belgium. Until an impartial investigation becomes possible no further proof than the claim made by the German Government can be produced.

As the French officers taken in Belgium are presumably in German detention camps, it would seem that Germany should first substantiate its defense by names, dates, and places, although even then the mere capture of French officers in Belgium after the invasion had begun does not necessarily indicate that they were in Belgium before the invasion.

Dr. von Mach adds in the reply, which he made in the New York Timesto an article contributed by the writer to that journal:

It is impossible to say here exactly what these proofs are which Germany possesses, and which for military reasons it has not yet been able to divulge.... This is an important question, and the answer must be left to The Supreme Court of Civilization. The weight of the evidence would seem to point to a justification of Germany. Yet no friend of Germany can find fault with those who would wish to defer a verdict until such time when Germany can present her complete proof to the world, and this may be when the war is over.

This naive suggestion, that the vital question of fact should be postponed, and in the meantime judgment should be entered for Germany, is refreshing in its novelty. Its only parallel was the contention of the celebrated Dr. Cook, who contended that the world should accept his claim as to the discovery of the North Pole and await the proofs later.

Professor von Mach, in his book, "What Germany Wants," further explains this dilatory defense and amplifies it in a manner that is certainly unusual in an historian. He recognizes that the speech of the German Chancellor in the Reichstag on August 4th, in which von Bethmann-Hollweg admitted that the action of Germany in invading Belgium was wrong and only justified it on the ground of self-preservation, was a virtual plea of guilty by Prussia of the crime, of which it stands indicted at the bar of the civilized world.

Germany's scholarly apologist, as amicus curi? then suggests that in criminal procedure, when a defendant pleads guilty, the Court often refuses to accept his plea, enters a plea of not guilty for him, and assigns counsel to defend the case. He therefore suggests that the Chancellor's plea of guilty should be disregarded and the Court should assign counsel.

One difficulty with the analogy is that courts do not ordinarily refuse to accept a plea of guilty. On the contrary, they accept it almost invariably, for why try the guilt of a man when he himself In the most formal way acknowledges it?

The only instance in which a court does show such consideration to a prisoner is when the defendant is both poor and ignorant. Then, and only then, with a fine regard for human right, is the procedure suggested by Prof. von Mach followed.

To this humiliating position, Professor von Mach as amicus curi 鎐 onsigns his great nation. For myself, as one who admires Germany and believes it to be much greater and truer than its ruling caste or its over-zealous apologists, I refuse to accept the justification of such an absurd and degrading analogy.

The blunt acknowledgment of the German Chancellor in the Reichstag, already quoted, is infinitely preferable to the disingenuous defenses of Germany's ardent but sophistical apologists. Fully recognizing the import of his words, von Bethmann-Hollweg, addressing the representatives of the German nation, put aside with admirable candor all these sophistical artifices and rested the defense of Germany upon the single contention that Germany was beset by powerful enemies and that it was a matter of necessity for her to perpetrate this "wrong" and in this manner to "hack her way through."

This defense is not even a plea of confession and avoidance. It is a plea of "Guilty" at the bar of the world. It has one merit. It does not add to the crime the aggravation of hypocrisy.

After the civilized world had condemned the invasion of Belgium with an unprecedented approach to unanimity, the German Chancellor rather tardily discovered that public opinion was still a vital force in the world and that the strategic results of the occupation of Belgium had not compensated for the moral injury. For this reason he framed five months after this crime against civilization a belated defense, which proved so unconvincing that the Bernhardi plea of military necessity is clearly preferable, as at least having the merit of candor.

After proclaiming to the world that the German Foreign Office had discovered in Brussels certain secret documents, which disclosed the fact that the neutrality of Belgium at the time of the invasion was a sham and after the civilized world had refused to accept this bald and unsupported assertion, as it had also refused to accept the spurious evidence of a well-known Arctic explorer, the German Foreign Office in December, 1914 published its alleged proofs.

The first purported to be a report of the Chief of the Belgian General Staff to the Minister of War and reported his conversations in 1906 with a military attach?of the British Legation in Brussels.

The second purported to be a report of similar conversations in 1912 between the same officials.

In an authorized statement, published on January 27, 1915, Sir Edward Grey states that there is no record of either of these negotiations in the English Foreign Office or the War Office; but this fact is not in itself conclusive and as there is no evidence that the documents were forged, their genuineness should be assumed in the absence of some more specific denial.

The documents, however, do not appreciably advance the cause of Germany, for they disclose on their face that the conversations were not binding on the Governments of England or Belgium but were simply an informal exchange of view between the officials, and what is far more to the purpose, the whole of the first conversation of April 10, 1906, was expressly based upon the statement that "the entry of the English into Belgium would take place only after the violation of our neutrality by Germany."

The second document also shows that the Belgian Chief of Staff expressly stated that any invasion of Belgium by England, made to repel a prior German invasion, could not take place without the express consent of Belgium, to be given when the occasion arose, and it is further evident that the statement of the English military attaché-clearly a subordinate official to define the foreign policy of a great Empire--expressly predicated his assumption, that England might disembark troops in Belgium, upon the statement that its object would be to repel a German invasion of Belgian territory.

If it be asked why England and Belgium were thus in 1906 and 1912 considering the contingency of a German invasion of Belgium and the method of effectually repelling it, the reply is obvious that such invasion, in the event of a war between Germany and France, was a commonplace of German military strategists. Of this purpose they made little, if any, concealment. The construction by Germany of numerous strategic railway lines on the Belgian frontier, which were out of proportion to the economic necessity of the territory, gave to Europe some indication of Germany's purpose and there could have been little doubt as to such intention, if Germany had not, through its Foreign Office, given, as previously shown, repeated and continuous assurances to Belgium that such was not its intention.

The German Chancellor--whose stupendous blunders of speech and action in this crisis will be the marvel of posterity--has further attempted to correct his record by two equally disingenuous defenses. Speaking to the Reichstag on December 2, 1914, he said:

When on the 4th of August I referred to the wrong which we were doing in marching through Belgium, it was not yet known for certain whether the Brussels Government in the hour of need would not decide after all to spare the country and to retire to Antwerp under protest. You remember that, after the occupation of Liege, at the request of our army leaders I repeated the offer to the Belgian Government. For military reasons it was absolutely imperative that at the time, about the 4th of August, the possibility for such a development should be kept open. Even then the guilt of the Belgian Government was apparent from many a sign, although I had not yet any positive documentary proofs at my disposal.

This is much too vague to excuse a great crime. The guilt of Belgium is said to be "apparent from many a sign," but what these signs are the Chancellor still fails to state. He admits that they were not documentary in character. If the guilt of Belgium had been so apparent to the Chancellor on August the 4th, when he made his confession of wrong doing in the Reichstag, then it is incredible that he would have made such an admission.

As to the overt acts of France, all that the Chancellor said in his speech of December 2 was "that France's plan of campaign was known to us and that it compelled us for reasons of self-preservation to march through Belgium." But it is again significant that, speaking nearly five months after his first public utterance on the subject and with a full knowledge that the world had visited its destructive condemnation upon Germany for its wanton attack upon Belgium, the Chancellor can still give no specific allegation of any overt act by France which justified the invasion. All that is suggested is a supposed "plan of campaign."

Following this unconvincing and plainly disingenuous speech, the Chancellor proceeded in an authorized newspaper interview on January 25, 1915 to state that his now famous--or infamous--remark about "the scrap of paper" had been misunderstood.

After stating that he felt a painful "surprise to learn that my phrase, 'a scrap of paper,' should have caused such an unfavorable impression on the United States," he proceeds to explain that in his now historic interview with the British Ambassador, he (von Bethmann-Hollweg) had spoken of the treaty not as a "scrap of paper" for Germany, but as an instrument which had become obsolete through Belgium's forfeiture of its neutrality and that Great Britain had quite other reasons for entering into the war, compared with which the neutrality treaty appeared to have only the value of a scrap of paper.

Let the reader here pause to note the twofold character of this defense.

It suggests that Germany's guaranty of Belgium's neutrality had become for Germany "a scrap of paper" because of Belgium's alleged forfeiture of its rights as a neutral nation, although at the time referred to the German Chancellor had not only asked the permission of Belgium to cross its territory but immediately before his interview with the British Ambassador he had publicly testified in his speech in the Reichstag to the justice of Belgium's protest.

The other and inconsistent suggestion is that, without respect to Belgium's rights under the treaty of 1839, the violation of its territory by Germany was not the cause of England's intervention; but obviously this hardly explains the German Chancellor's contemptuous reference to the long standing and oft repeated guaranty of Belgium's neutrality as merely a "scrap of paper."

Having thus somewhat vaguely suggested a twofold defense, the Chancellor, without impeaching the accuracy of Goschen's report of the interview, then proceeded to state that the conversation in question took place immediately after his speech in the Reichstag, in which, as stated, he had admitted the justice of Belgium's protest against the violation of its territory, and he adds that,

when I spoke, I already had certain indications but no absolute proof upon which to base a public accusation that Belgium long before had abandoned its neutrality in its relations with England. Nevertheless I took Germany's responsibilities toward the neutral States so seriously that I spoke frankly of the wrong committed by Germany.

If the German Chancellor is truthful in his statement that on August the 4th, when he spoke in the Reichstag and an hour later had his conversation with

Goschen, he had "certain indications" that Belgium had forfeited its rights as an independent nation by hostile acts, then the German Chancellor took such a serious view of "Germany's responsibilities" that, without any necessity or justification, he indicted his country at the bar of the whole world of a flagrant wrong. If he could not at that time justify the act of the German General Staff, he should at least have been silent, but, according to his incredible statement, although he had these "certain indications" and thus knew that Germany, in invading Belgium, was simply attacking an already hostile country, he deliberately explains, not only to his nation but to the whole world, that such invasion was a wrong and had no justification in international law. How can any reasonable man, whose eyes are not blinded with the passions of the hour, accept this explanation?

It is even more remarkable that immediately following the session of the Reichstag, when he had his interview with Goschen, the German Chancellor never suggested in his own defense or that of his country, that he had "certain indications," which justified the action that day taken, although he then knew that, unless he could justify it, England would immediately join the already powerful foes of Germany.

The reader need only reread Goschen's report of that interview (ante, p. 214) to know how disingenuous this belated explanation is. With the whole world ringing with the infamous phrase, the German Chancellor, after five months of reflection, can only make this pitiful defense. Its acceptance subjects even the most credulous to a severe strain. It exhausts the limit of gullibility.

The defense wholly ignores the fact that the Chancellor had previously sought to bribe England to condone in advance the invasion of Belgium by Germany, and that Germany had also coerced Luxemburg into a passive acquiescence in a similar invasion, and there is as yet no pretense that Luxemburg had failed in its obligation of neutrality.

Should the judgment of the civilized world turn from the terrible fate of Belgium and consider the wrong that was done to Luxemburg, then the German Chancellor may, unless better advised, frame further maladroit excuses with reference to that country.

All these explanations, as senseless as they are false, and savoring more of the tone of a criminal court then that of an imperial chancellery, should shock those who admire historic Germany. They are unworthy of so great a nation. Bismarck would never have stooped to such pitiful and transparent deception. The blunt candor of Maximilian Harden, which we have already quoted on page 12, is infinitely preferable and the position of Germany at the bar of the civilized world will improve, when its maladroit Chancellor has the courage and the candor to say, as Harden did, that all this was done because Germany regarded it as for its vital interests and because "we willed it."

Unless our boasted civilization is the thinnest veneering of barbarism; unless the law of the world is in fact only the ethics of the rifle and the conscience of the cannon; unless mankind, after uncounted centuries, has made no real advance in political morality beyond that of the cave dweller, then this answer of Germany cannot satisfy the "decent respect to the opinions of mankind." It is the negation of all that civilization stands for.

Belgium has been crucified in the face of the world. Its innocence of any offense, until it was attacked, is too clear for argument. Its voluntary immolation to preserve its solemn guarantee of neutrality will "plead like angels, trumpet-tongued, against the deep damnation of its taking off."

It may be questioned whether, since the fall of Poland, Civilization has been stirred to more profound pity and intense indignation than by this wanton outrage. Pity, radiating to the utmost corners of the world by the "sightless couriers of the air,"

"Shall blow the horrid deed in every eye That tears shall drown the wind."

Was it also, as with Macbeth, a case of

"Vaulting ambition which o'erleaps itself And falls on the other"?

Time will tell.

Had Germany not invaded Belgium, it is an even chance that England would not have intervened, at least at the beginning of the war.

Germany could have detached a relatively small part of its army to defend its highly fortified Western frontier, and leaving France to waste its strength on frontal attacks on that almost impregnable line of defense, Germany with the bulk of its army and that of Austria could have made a swift drive at Russia.

Is it not possible that that course would have yielded better results than the fiasco, which followed the fruitless drive at Paris?

If Germany succeeds, it will claim that "nothing succeeds like success," and to the disciples of Treitschke and Bernhardi this will be a sufficing answer.

If it fail, posterity will be at a loss to determine which blundered the worst, the German Foreign Office or its General Staff, its diplomats or its generals.

CHAPTER X

THE JUDGMENT OF THE WORLD

The record has now been laid before the reader in all its essential details. The witnesses for the different countries have taken the stand and we have their respective contentions in their own words. Czar, Emperor, and King, as well as Prime Minister, Chancellor, and Ambassador, have testified as to the fateful events, which preceded the outbreak of the war, with a fullness of detail, to which history presents few parallels. The evidence which Germany and Austria have suppressed does not prevent the determination of the issue.

It is a great tribute to the force of public opinion and a clear recognition that the conscience of mankind does exist as something more than a visionary abstraction, that the secrets of diplomacy have been laid bare by most of the contending nations, and that there is an earnest desire on the part of all of them to justify their conduct respectively at the bar of the civilized world.

Even more impressive to the sincere friends of peace is the significant fact that concurrently with the most amazing display of physical force that the world has ever known has come a direct appeal by the belligerent nations to the neutral States, and especially to the United States, not for practical cooperation in the hostilities but for moral sympathy.

All past wars are insignificant in dimensions in comparison with this. The standing army of the Roman Empire, according to the estimate of Gibbon, did not exceed 400,000, and guarded that mighty Empire from the Euphrates to the Thames. The grand army of Napoleon, which was supposed to mark the maximum of human effort in the art of war and with which he crossed a century ago the Niemen, did not exceed 700,000. To-day at least fifteen millions of men are engaged in a titanic struggle, with implements of destruction, to which all past devices in the science of destruction are insignificant.

Apparently, therefore, the ideals of the pacificist are little better than a rainbow, a rainbow of promise, perhaps, but still a rainbow, formed by the rays of God's justice shining through the tears of human pity.

But when, in contrast to this amazing display of physical power, there is contrasted an equally unprecedented desire on the part of the contending nations to justify their case at the bar of public opinion and to gain the moral sympathy of the neutral States, then it is seen that the "decent respect to the opinions of mankind" is still a mighty factor in human affairs, and the question as to the judgment of the world, upon the moral issues raised by this great controversy, becomes not merely of academic but of great practical interest.

What that judgment will be it is not difficult to determine, for the evidence in the case can admit of but one conclusion. It may be, as Mr. George Bernard Shaw says, that in the contending nations, the ears are too greatly deafened by the roar of the cannon and the eyes too blinded by the smoke of battle, to reach a dispassionate conclusion. But in the neutral States of the world, and especially in that greatest of all the neutral Powers, the United States of America, a judgment has been pronounced that is unmistakable.

The great Republic is more free than any other nation to reach a just conclusion "without fear, favor, or affection." Without alliances with any Power and with no practical interest in the European balance of power, itself composed of men of all the contending nations, it can, above every other people, proceed to judgment, "with malice toward none and with charity for all."

It is a tribute to its unique position among the nations of the world that from the beginning of the war each of the contending Powers has invoked its judgment. The Kaiser, the President of the French Republic, and the King of Belgium have each in an especial way sought its moral support, while to the other nations the question of the attitude of the United States has been one of practical and recognized importance.

If the United States is thus a moral arbiter in the greatest war of history, its judgment is now, and may hereafter increasingly become, a potential factor of great significance.

The nature of that judgment is already apparent to all men. The people of the United States, numbering nearly one hundred millions, have reached, with an amazing approach to unanimity, certain clear and definite conclusions.

These conclusions maybe summarized as follows:

1. That Germany and Austria in a time of profound peace secretly concerted to impose their will upon Europe in a matter affecting the balance of power. Whether in so doing they intended to precipitate a European war to determine the hegemony of Europe is not satisfactorily established, although their whole course of conduct suggests this as a possibility. They made war almost inevitable by (a) issuing an ultimatum that was grossly unreasonable and disproportionate to any grievance that Austria may have had, and (b) in giving to Servia and Europe insufficient time to consider the rights and obligations of all interested nations.

2. That Germany had at all times the power to induce Austria to preserve a reasonable and conciliatory course, but at no time effectively exerted its influence. On the contrary, it certainly abetted, and possibly instigated, Austria in its unreasonable course.

3. That England, France, Italy, and Russia throughout the diplomatic controversy sincerely worked for peace, and in this spirit not only overlooked the original misconduct of Austria but made every reasonable concession in the hope of preserving peace.

4. That Austria, having mobilized its army, Russia was reasonably justified in mobilizing its forces. Such act of mobilization is the right of any sovereign State, and as long as the Russian armies did not cross the border or take any aggressive action, no other nation had any just right to complain, each having the same right to make similar preparations.

5. That Germany, in abruptly declaring war against Russia for failure to demobilize, when the other Powers had offered to make any reasonable concession and peace parleys were still in progress, precipitated the war.

6. That the invasion of Belgium by Germany was without any provocation and in violation of Belgium's inherent rights as a sovereign State. The sanctity of its territory does not depend exclusively upon the Treaty of 1839 or The Hague Convention, but upon fundamental and axiomatic principles of international law. These treaties were simply declaratory of Belgium's rights as a sovereign nation and simply reaffirmed by a special covenant the duty of Germany and the other Powers to respect the neutrality of Belgium.

7. England was justified in its declaration of war upon Germany, not only because of its direct interests in the neutrality of Belgium, but also because of the ethical duty of the strong nations to protect the weak upon adequate occasion from indefensible wrong. Apart from this general ethical justification, England was, under the Treaty of 1839, under an especial obligation to defend the neutrality of Belgium, and had it failed to respect that obligation it would have broken its solemn covenant.

If they are "thrice armed" who have their "quarrel just," then England, France, Russia, and Belgium can await with confidence, not merely the immediate issue of the titanic conflict, but also the equally important judgment of history.

EPILOGUE

On the evening of July 31, 1914, the author reached Basle. The rapid progress of events, narrated in this volume, suggested the wisdom of continuing the journey to Paris that night, but as I wanted to see the tomb of Erasmus in the Basle Cathedral I determined to break my long journey from St. Moritz.

It seemed a fitting time to make a pilgrimage to the last resting-place of the great humanist philosopher of Rotterdam and Louvain, for in that prodigious upheaval of the sixteenth century, which has passed into history as the Reformation, Erasmus was the one noble spirit who looked with a tolerant and philosophical mind upon both parties to the great controversy. He suffered the fate of the conservative in a radical time, and as the great storm convulsed Europe the author of the Praise of Folly probably said on more than one occasion: "A plague o' both your houses." Nearly four centuries have passed since he joined the "silent majority," between whom is no quarreling, and the desolated Louvain, which he loved, is to-day in its ruins a standing witness that immeasurable folly still rules the darkened counsels of men.

As I reached Basle and saw the spires of the Cathedral rising above the Rhine, it seemed to me that the great convulsion, which was then rocking all Europe with seismic violence, was the greatest since that of the French Revolution and might have as lasting results as the great schism of the sixteenth century.

I was not fated to see the tomb, for when I reached my hotel the facilities of civilization had broken down so abruptly that if I did not wish to be interned in Switzerland I must leave early on the following morning for Paris. Transportation had almost entirely collapsed, communication was difficult, and credit itself was so strained that "mine host" of the Three Kings was disposed to look askance even at gold.

Our journey took us to France by way of Delle. Twenty-four hours after we passed that frontier town, German soldiers entered and blew out the brains of a French custom-house officer, thus the first victim in the greatest war that the world has ever known.

As we journeyed from Basle to Paris on that last day of July the fair fields of France never looked more beautiful. In the gleaming summer sun they made a new "field of the cloth of gold," and the hayricks looked like the aureate tents of a mighty army. It was harvest time, but already the laborers had deserted their fields which, although "white unto the harvest," seemed bereft of the tillers. Some had left the bounty of nature to join in the harvest of death. From the high pasture lands of the Alps the herdsmen at the ringing of the village church bells had left their herds and before night had fallen were on their way to the front.

At Belfort the station was crowded with French troops and an elderly French couple came into our compartment. The eyes of the wife were red with weeping, while the man sank into his seat and with his head upon his breast gazed moodily into vacancy. They had just parted with their son, who had joined the colors. I stood for a time with this French gentleman in the corridor of the train, but as he could not speak English or German and I could not speak French, it was impossible for us to communicate the intense and tragical thoughts that were passing through our minds. Suddenly he pointed to the smiling harvest fields, by which we passed so swiftly, and said "Perdu! perdu!" This word of tragical import could have been applied to all civilization as well.

The night of our arrival in Paris I fully expected to see a half a million Frenchmen parading the streets and enthusiastically cheering for war and crying, as in 1870, "?Berlin!" I was to witness an extraordinary transformation of a great nation. An unusual silence brooded over the city. A few hundred people paraded the chief avenues, crying "down with war!", while a separate crowd of equal size sang the national hymn. With these exceptions there was no cheering or enthusiasm, such as I would have expected from my preconceived idea of French excitability. Men spoke in undertones, with a quiet but subdued intensity of feeling rather than with frenzied enthusiasm.

With a devotion that was extraordinary and a pathetically brave submission to a possible fate, they seemed to be sternly resolved to die to the last man, if necessary, in defense of their noble nation. Although I subsequently saw in the thrilling days of mobilization many thousands of soldiers pass through the railroad stations on their way to the front, I never heard the rumble of a drum or saw the waving of regimental colors.

No sacrifice seemed to be too great, whether it was asked of man, woman, or child. The spirit of materialism for the time being vanished. The newspapers shrunk to a single sheet and all commercial advertisements disappeared. Theaters, art galleries, museums, libraries, closed their doors. Upon some streets nearly every shop was closed, with the simple but eloquent placard "Gone to join the colors." The French people neither exulted, boasted, nor complained. The only querulous element was a small minority of the large body of American tourists, so suddenly caught in a terrific storm of human passions, who seemed to feel that this Red Sea of blood should part until they could walk dry-shod to the shore of safety.

In Germany similar scenes were enacted and a like spirit of courage and self-sacrifice was shown.

It is a reflection upon civilization that two nations, each so brave, heroic, and self-sacrificing, should, without their consent and by the miserable and iniquitous folly of scheming statesmen and diplomats, be plunged into a war, of which no man can see the end and which has already swept away the flower of their manhood.

One great lesson of this conflict may be that no aggressive war ought to be initiated unless the policy of that war is first submitted to the masses of the people, upon whom the burdens in the last analysis fall and who must pay the dreadful penalty with their treasure and their lives.

If the policy of this war had been submitted by a referendum to the Austrian and German peoples with a full statement of the facts of the Servian controversy, would they not have rejected a form of arbitrament, which creates but does not settle questions, convinces no one, and only sows the seeds of greater hatred for future and richer harvests of death? If the be-ribboned diplomats and decorated generals of the General Staffs at Berlin and Vienna had been without power to precipitate this war, unless they themselves were willing to occupy the trenches on the firing line, this war might never have been.

* * * * *

Nearly five months have passed since that summer day, when I passed through smiling harvest fields from the mountains to the Seine. The trenches, in which innumerable brave men are writing with their blood the records of their statesmen's follies, are filled with snow. The blackest Christmas Eve within the memory of living man has come and gone, perhaps the blackest, since in the stillness of the night there fell upon the wondering ears of the shepherds the gracious refrain of "Peace on earth, good will among men." On that night devout German soldiers sang in their trenches in Flanders and along the Vistula the hymn of Christmas Eve, "Stille Nacht, heilige Nacht."

Was this unconscious mockery, an expression of invincible faith, or a reversion from habit to the gentler associations of childhood? The spirit of Christmas was not wholly dead, for it is narrated that these brave men in English and German trenches on this saddest of Christmas Eves declared for a few hours of their own volition a Christmas truce.

"Some say that ever 'gainst that season comes Wherein our Saviour's birth is celebrated The bird of dawning singeth all night long, And then, they say, no spirit dare stir abroad, The nights are wholesome, then no planets strike, So hallowed and so gracious is the time."

There is not between the men in one trench and those in another, each seeking the speediest opportunity to kill the other, any personal quarrel. On occasion they even fraternize, only to resume the work of mutual extermination. They would not have quarreled, if the Berchtolds, the von Bethmann-Hollwegs, and the von Jagows had had sufficient loyalty to civilization to submit any possible grievance, which either had, to the judgment of Europe.

A spectacle more ghastly than this "far-flung battle line" has never been witnessed since the world began, for these soldiers in gray or khaki are not savages but are beings of an advanced civilization. Their fighting can have in method none of the old-time chivalry, such as was witnessed at Fontenoy when the French commander courteously invited his English rival to fire first. The present is a chemical, mechanical war, than which no circle in Dante's Inferno is more horribly repellent.

When was better justified the terrible but beautiful imagery in Milton's poem of The Nativity, when he says of Nature:

"Only with speeches fair She woos the gentle air To hide her guilty front with innocent snow, And on her naked shame Pollute with sinful blame The saintly veil of maiden white to throw; Confounded that her Maker's eyes Should look so near upon her foul deformities."

The snow cannot hide the horrors of the present conflict. Even night, in other wars more merciful, no longer throws its sable mantle of mercy over the dying and the dead. By the use of powerful searchlights the work of destruction continues. As though the surface of the earth were no longer sufficient for this malignant exercise of the genius of man, the heavens above and the waters under the earth have become at length the battlefields of the nations. Even from the infinite azure falls

".... a ghastly dew From the nations' airy navies, grappling in the central blue."

Can all history afford a parallel in malignity to the submarine, which, having sunk one vessel with all its human lives, calmly awaits, with its periscope projecting above the water like the malignant eye of a devil fish, the arrival of rescuing ships to sink them also?

Was the gracious refrain of "Peace on earth, good will among men," merely a mockery of man's hope, making of his civilization a mere mirage? Will

"Caesar's spirit ranging for revenge With Ate from his side come hot from Hell"--

forever crucify afresh and put to an open shame the gentle Galilean?

The angelic song of Bethlehem was neither the statement of a fact nor even a prophecy. In its true translation it was the statement of a profound moral truth, upon which in the last analysis the pacification of humanity must depend. The great promise was "Peace on earth to men of good will."

Peace to the pacific, that was the great message. For all others the great Teacher had but one prediction and that was "the distress of nations, ... men's hearts failing them for fear." Until civilization can grasp the truth that there can be no peace until there is among all nations a spirit of conciliation and a common desire of justice, the cause of peace can be little more than a beautiful dream. Hague conventions, international tribunals, and agreements to arbitrate, while minimizing the causes of war and affording the machinery for the pacific adjustment of justiciable questions, will yet prove altogether ineffectual, irrespective of the size of the parchment, the imposing character of the seals, or the length of the red tape, unless the nations which execute them have sufficient loyalty to civilization to ask only that which seems just and to submit any disputable question to the pacific adjustment of an impartial tribunal.

I appreciate that some questions are not justiciable and cannot be arbitrated. The historic movements of races, like those of glaciers, cannot be stopped by mortal hands, and yet even these slow-moving masses of ice are stayed by an Invisible Hand and melt at length into gentle and fructifying streams. To create the universal state and to develop a spirit of paramount loyalty to it affords the only solution of this seemingly insoluble problem.

History affords no more striking illustration of this fact than the present war. Each of the contending nations was pledged to peace. All of the greater ones were signatories to the Hague Convention, but as the chain can never be stronger than its weakest link, the pacific efforts of England, France, and Russia to adjust a purely justiciable question by negotiation and mediation wholly failed because Austria and Germany had determined to test the mastery of Europe by an appeal to the sword. The fundamental cause of the conflict was their lack of loyalty to civilization, due to a misguided and perverted spirit of excessive nationalism.

Until with the slow-moving progress of mankind the greater unit of the Universal State can be created, it should be the common and equal concern of all nations, not merely to defeat this primitive appeal to brute force but to make impossible the recurrence of such an iniquitous reversion to barbarism. To do this, while any nation unjustly appeals to force, force is unhappily necessary, but there would be few occasions to repel force by force if there were sufficient solidarity in mankind to make it the common concern of the civilized world to suppress promptly and effectually any disturber of its peace.

If the present wanton attack upon the very foundations of civilization had been regarded as the common concern of all nations, it would never have taken place and might never occur again. To prevent such recurrence, thoughtful men of all nations should cooperate, so that when the present titanic struggle is over, an earnest and universal effort can be made to create such a compact between the civilized nations as will insure cooperative effort when any nation attempts to apply the torch of war to the stately edifice of civilization. May not this great war prove the supreme travail of humanity, whereof this nobler era will be born?

It should be the especial duty of the United States to lead in this onward movement. It has been in no small measure the liberator of mankind. Let it now be its pacificator! Can it do so in any better spirit than that voiced by one of the noblest of its Presidents at the close of another gigantic conflict, of which he was to be the last and greatest martyr, when he said:

With malice toward none, with charity for all, with firmness in the right as God gives us to see the right, let us strive to finish the work we are in; to bind up the nation's wounds; to care for him who shall have borne the battle, and for his widow and orphan; and to do all which may achieve and cherish a just and lasting peace.

###

www.ingramcontent.com/pod-product-compliance
Lightning Source LLC
Chambersburg PA
CBHW060335290526
45793CB00003B/629